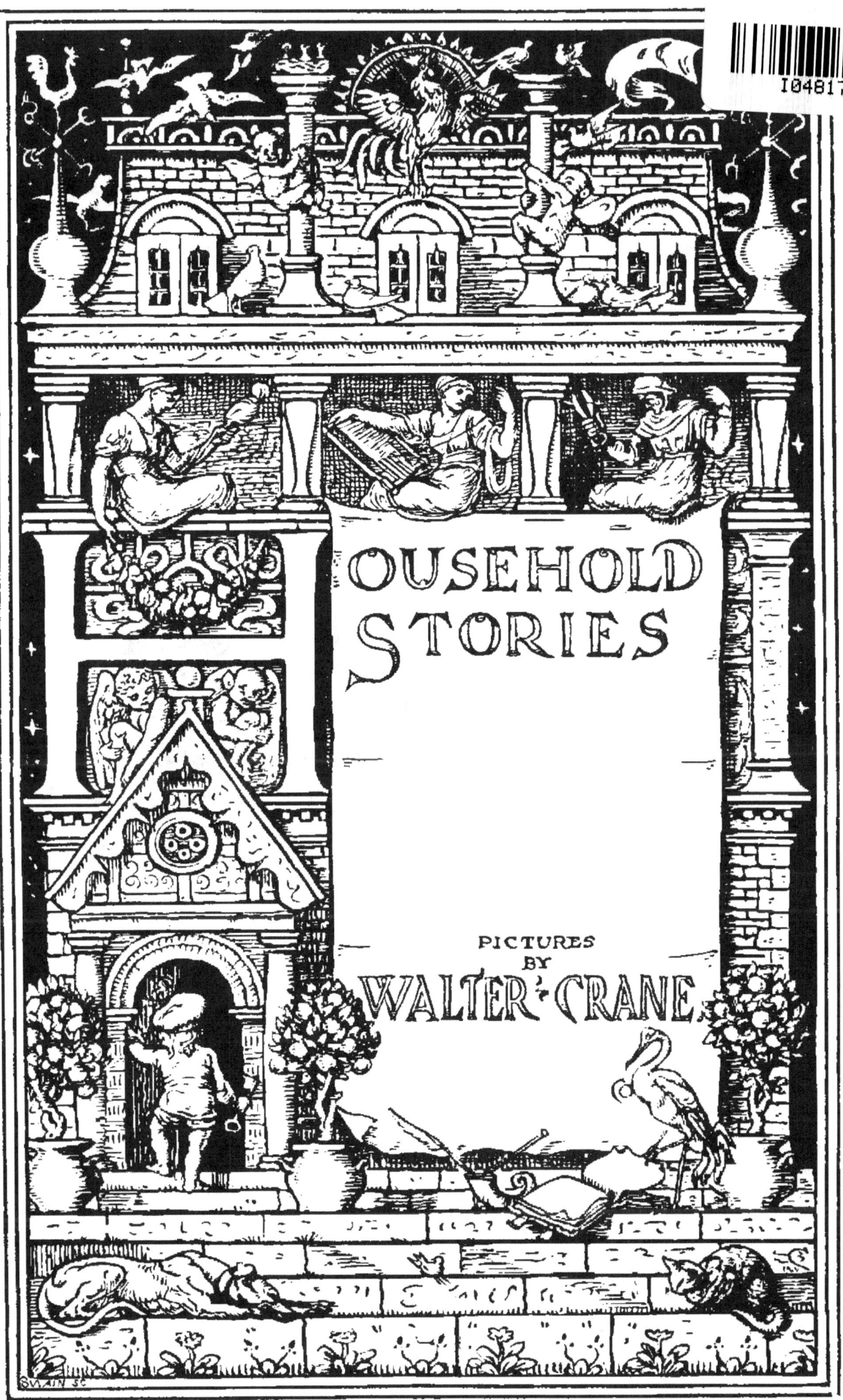

OUSEHOLD STORIES

PICTURES BY
WALTER CRANE

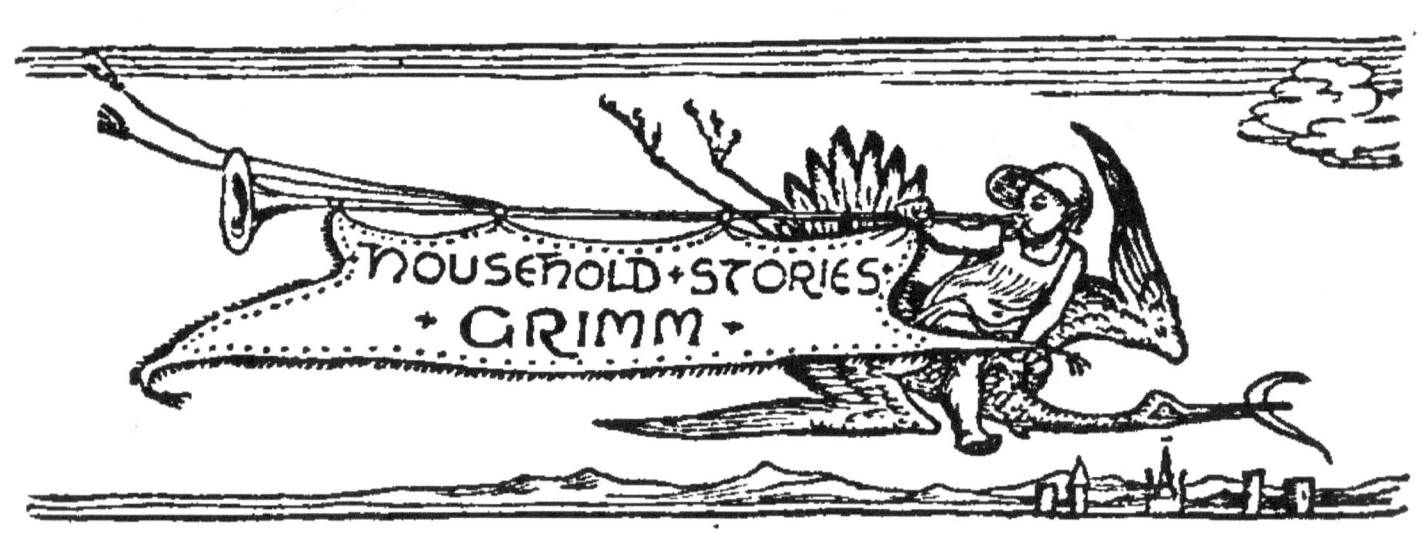

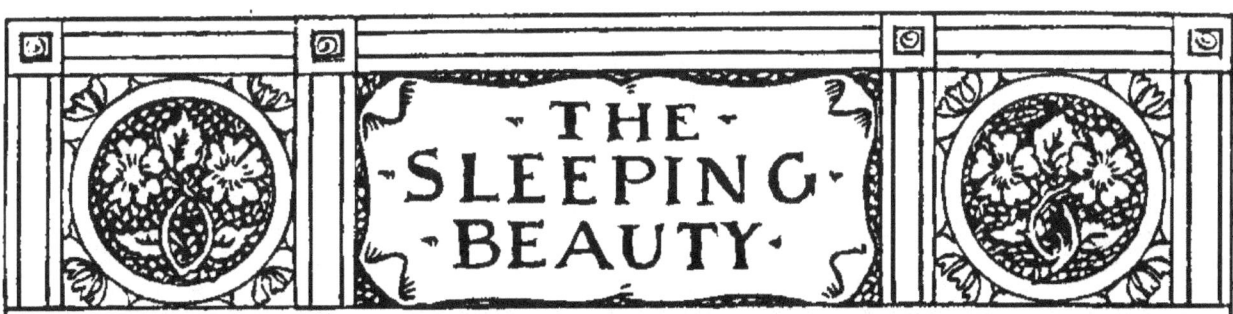

·THE· SLEEPING· BEAUTY·

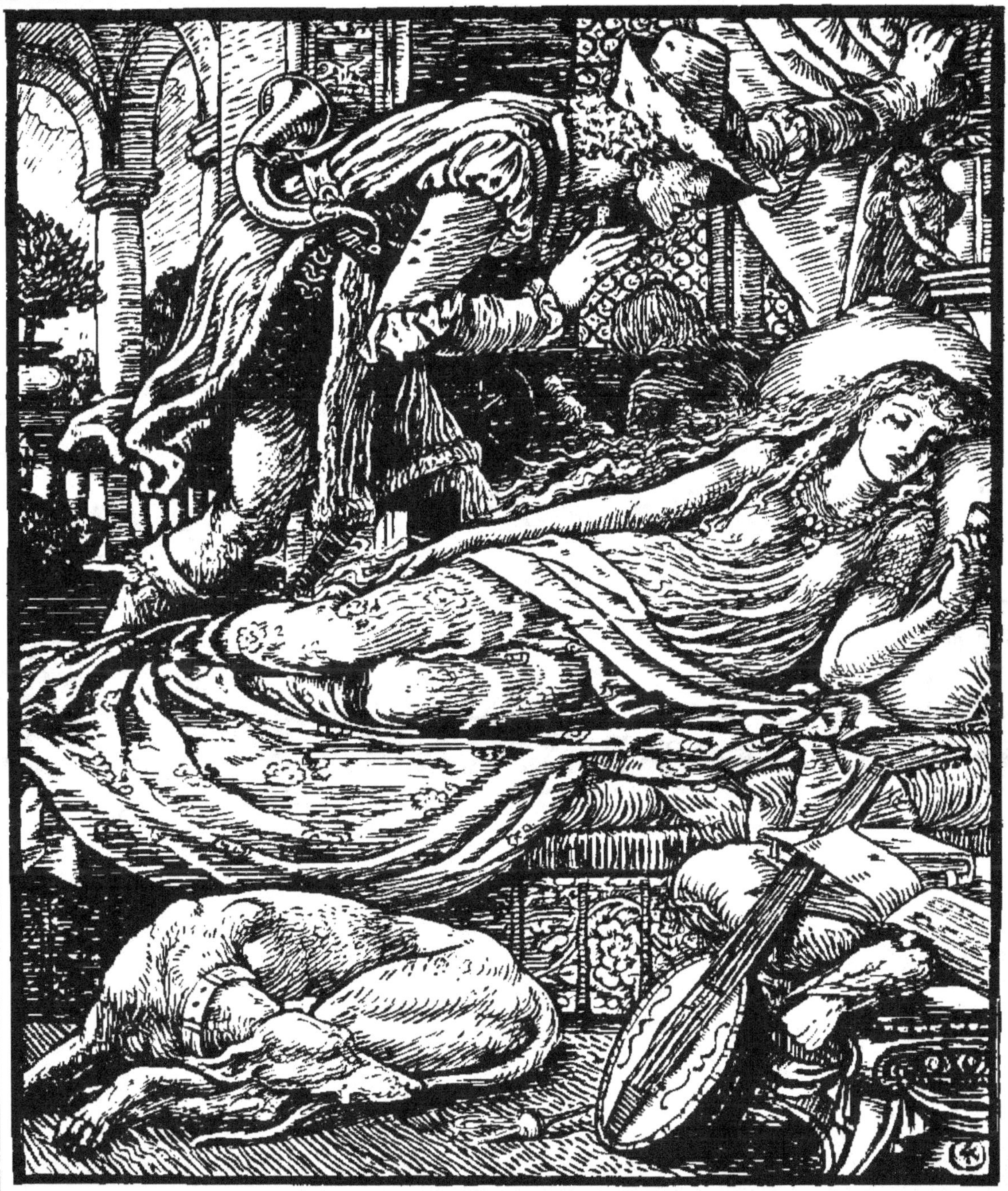

·"AT·LAST·HE·CAME·TO·THE·
·TOWER·&·OPENED·THE·DOOR·
·OF·THE·LITTLE·ROOM·WHERE·
·ROSAMOND·LAY·

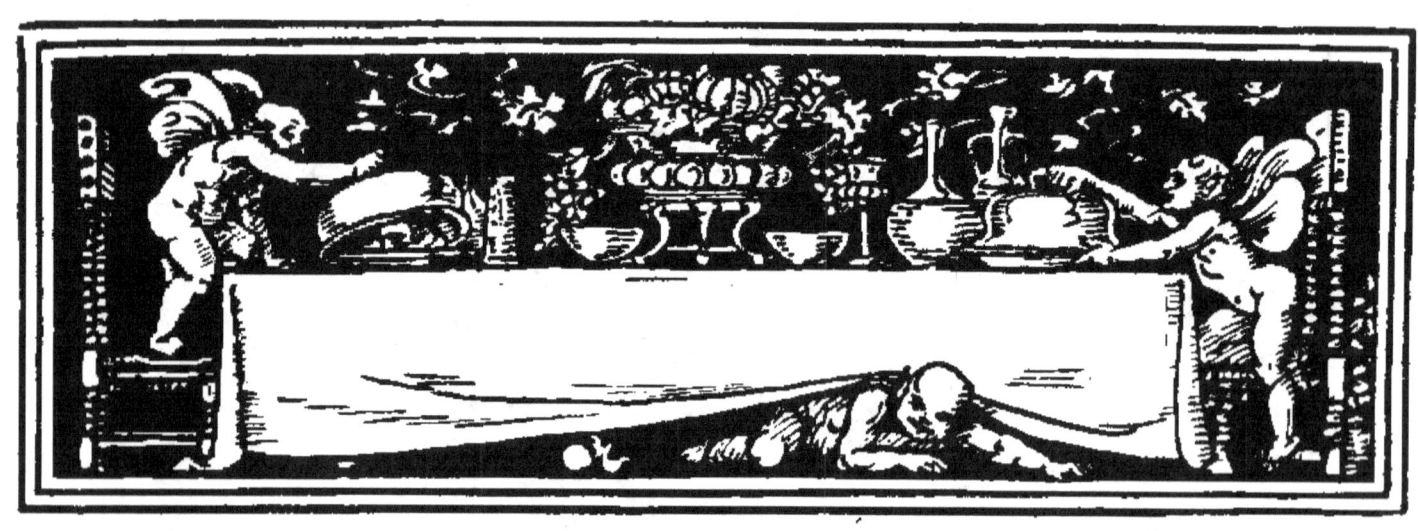

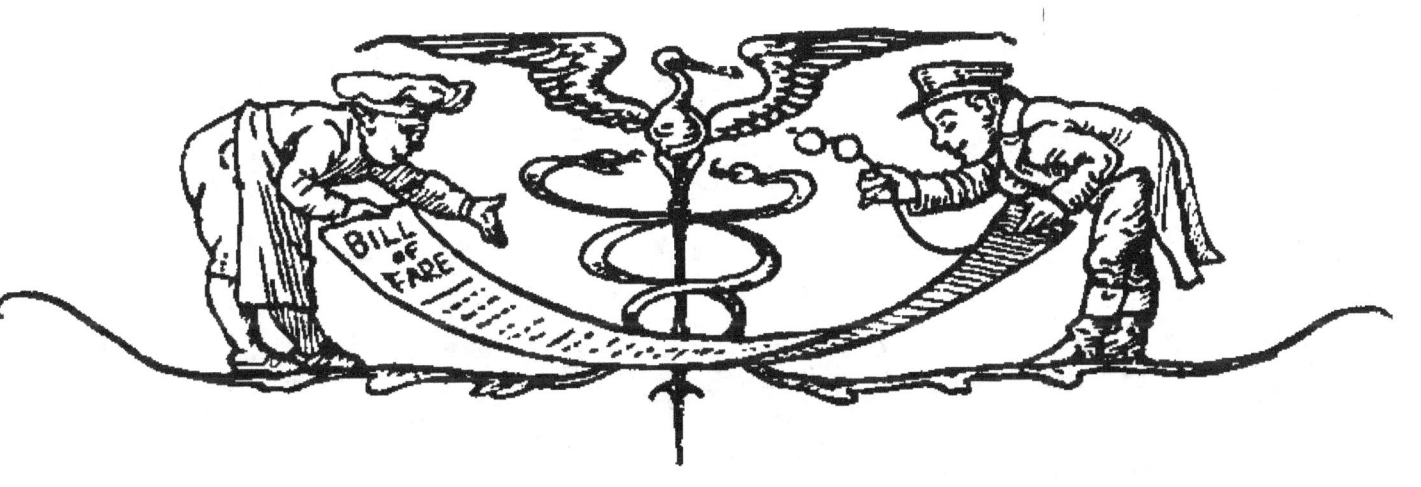

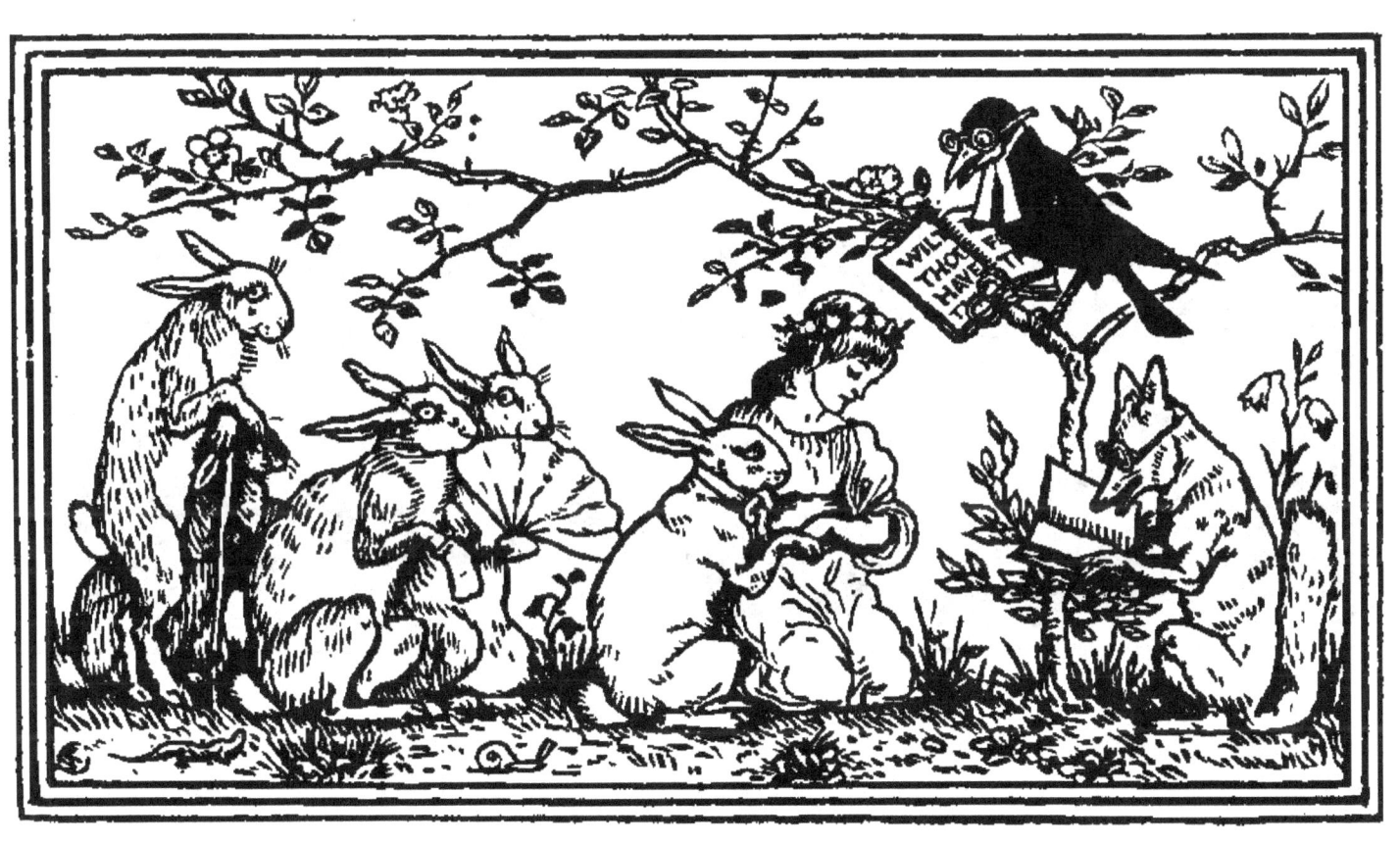

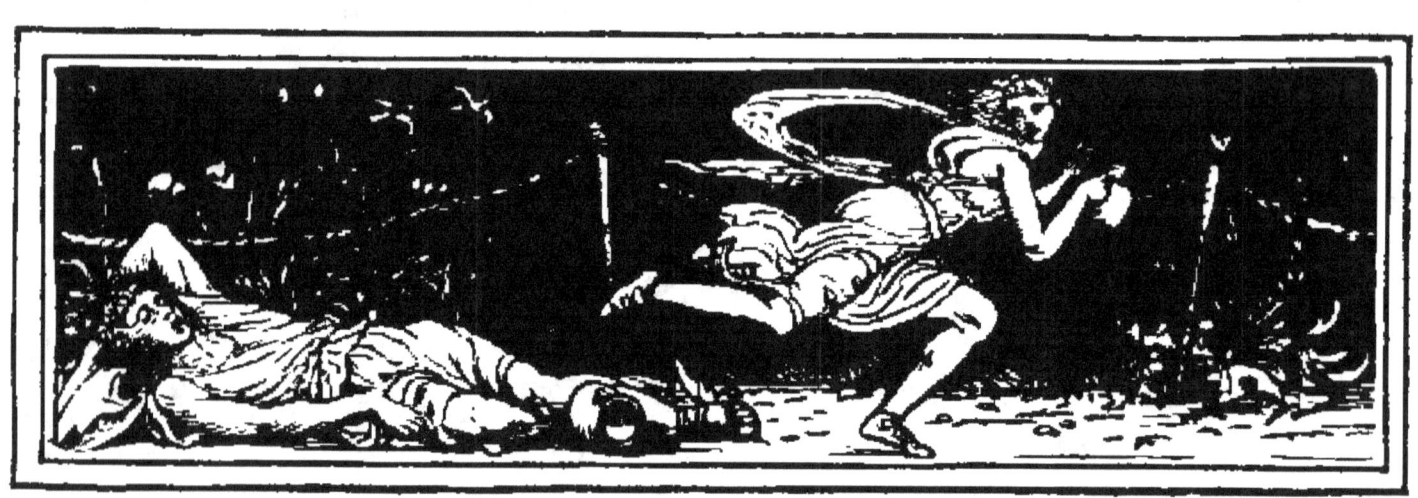

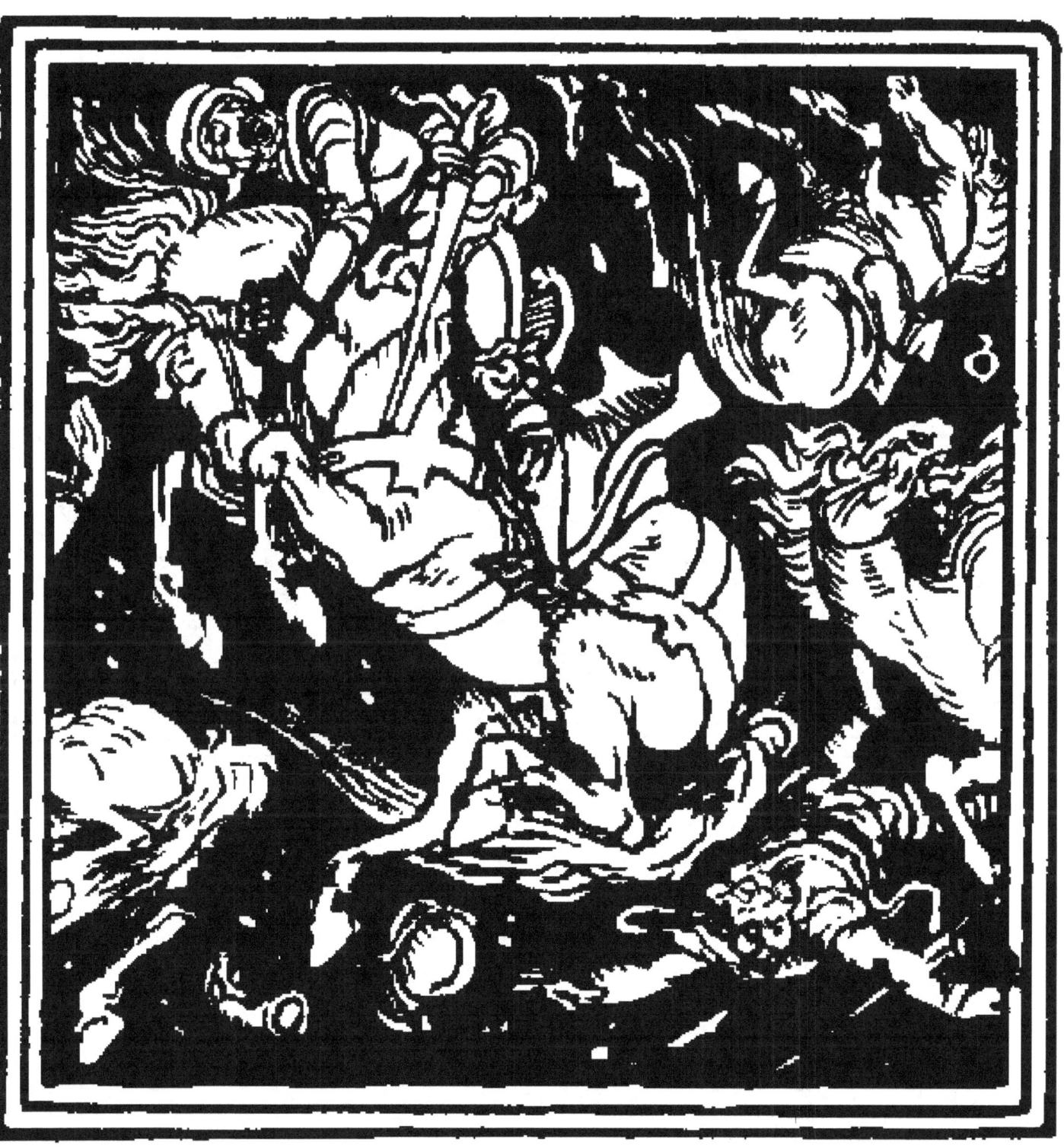

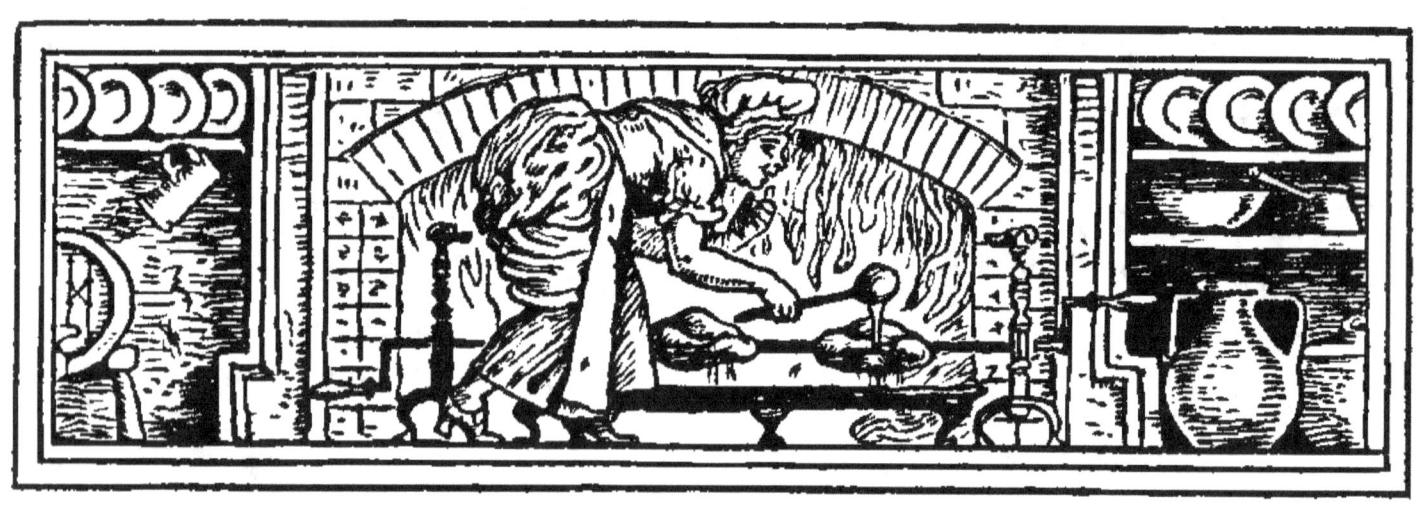

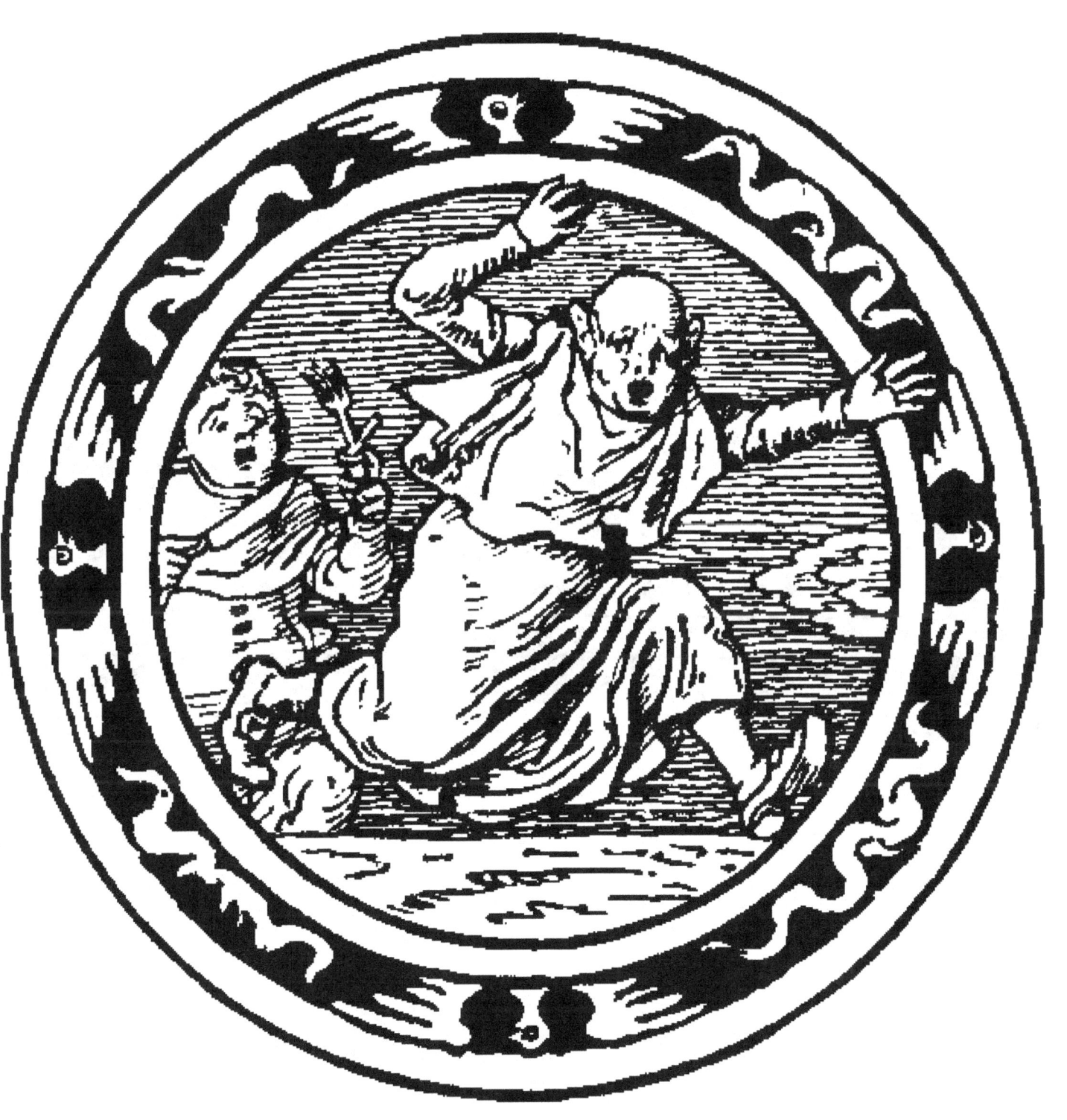

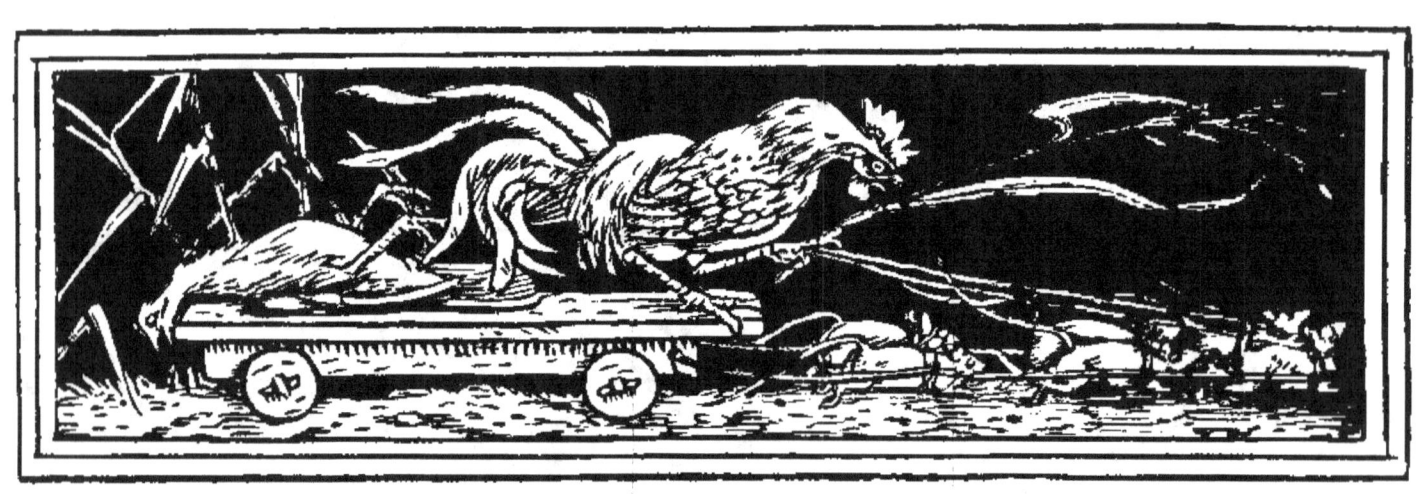

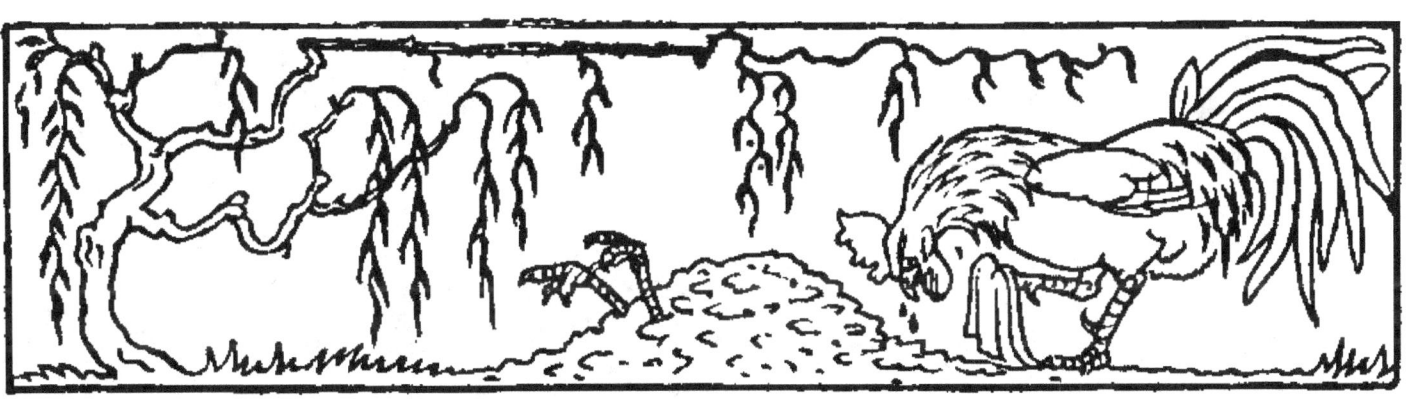

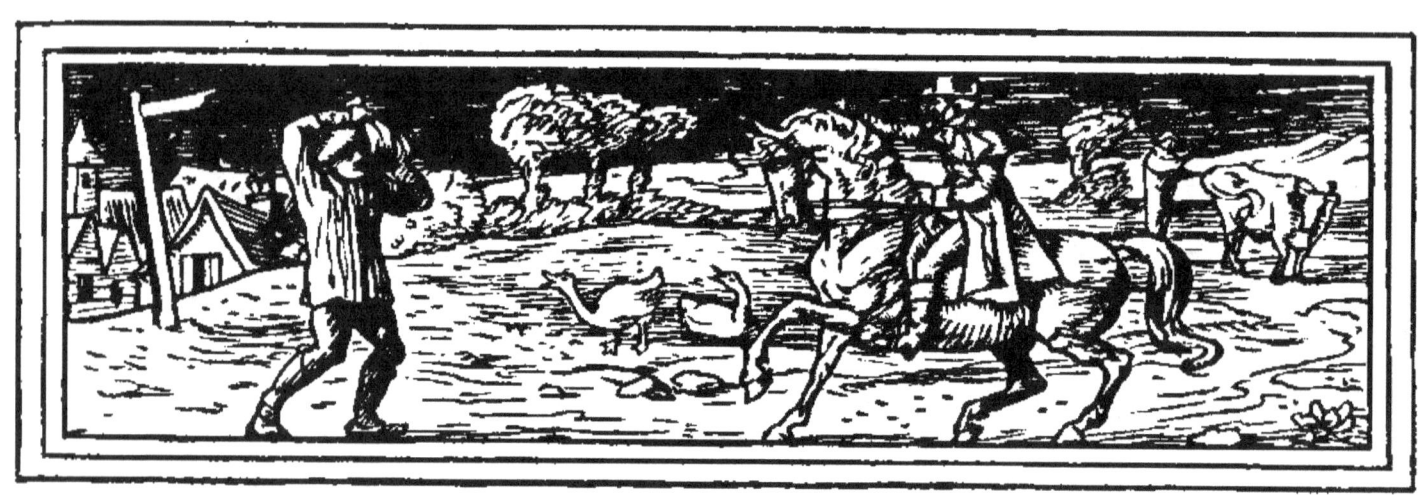

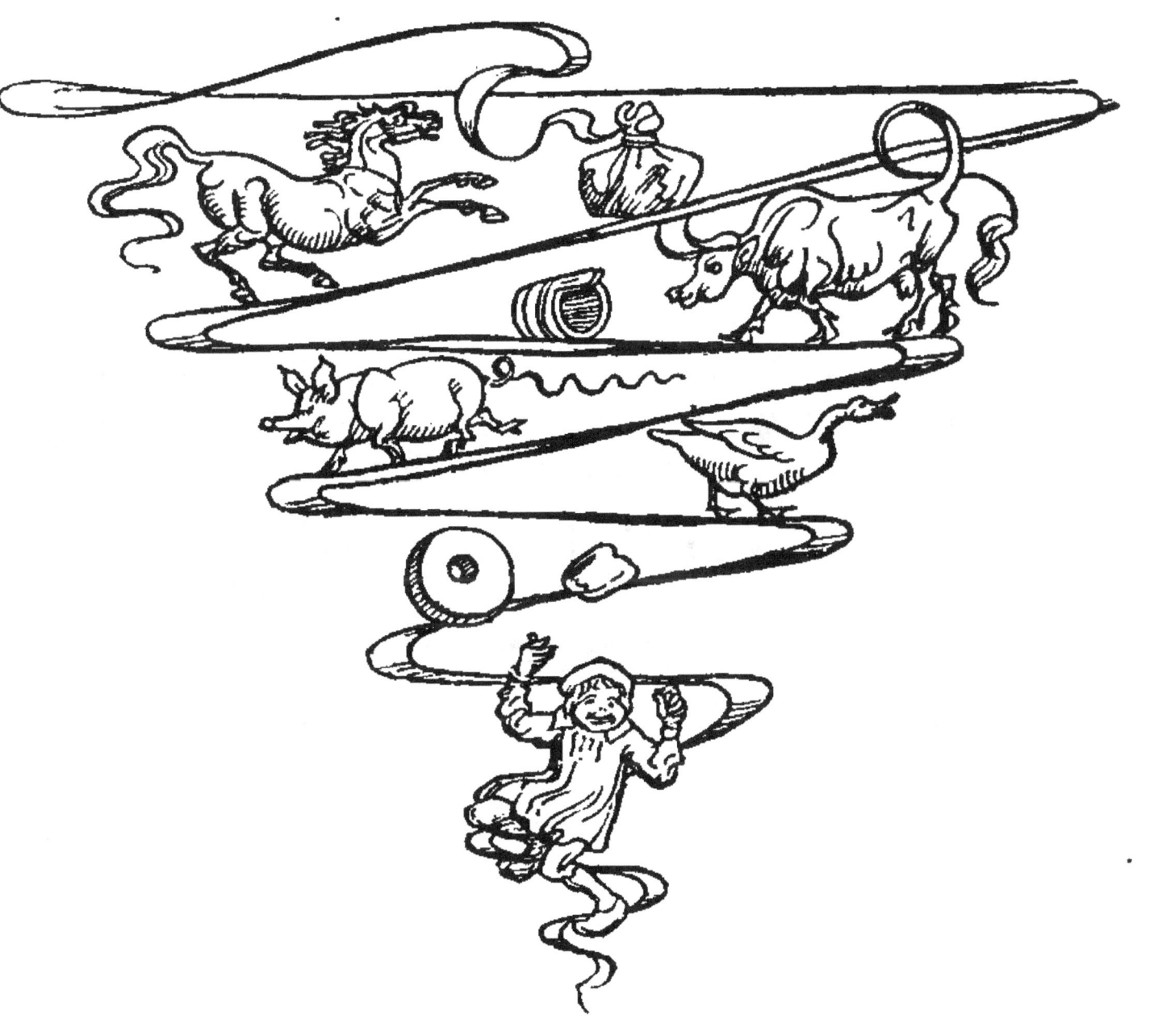

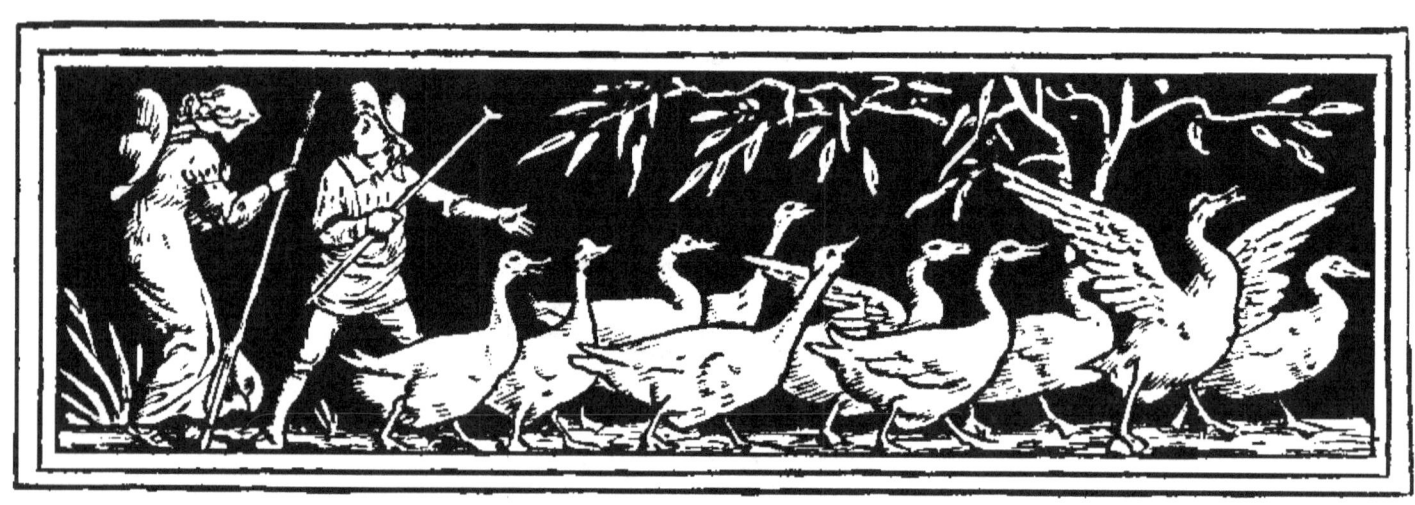

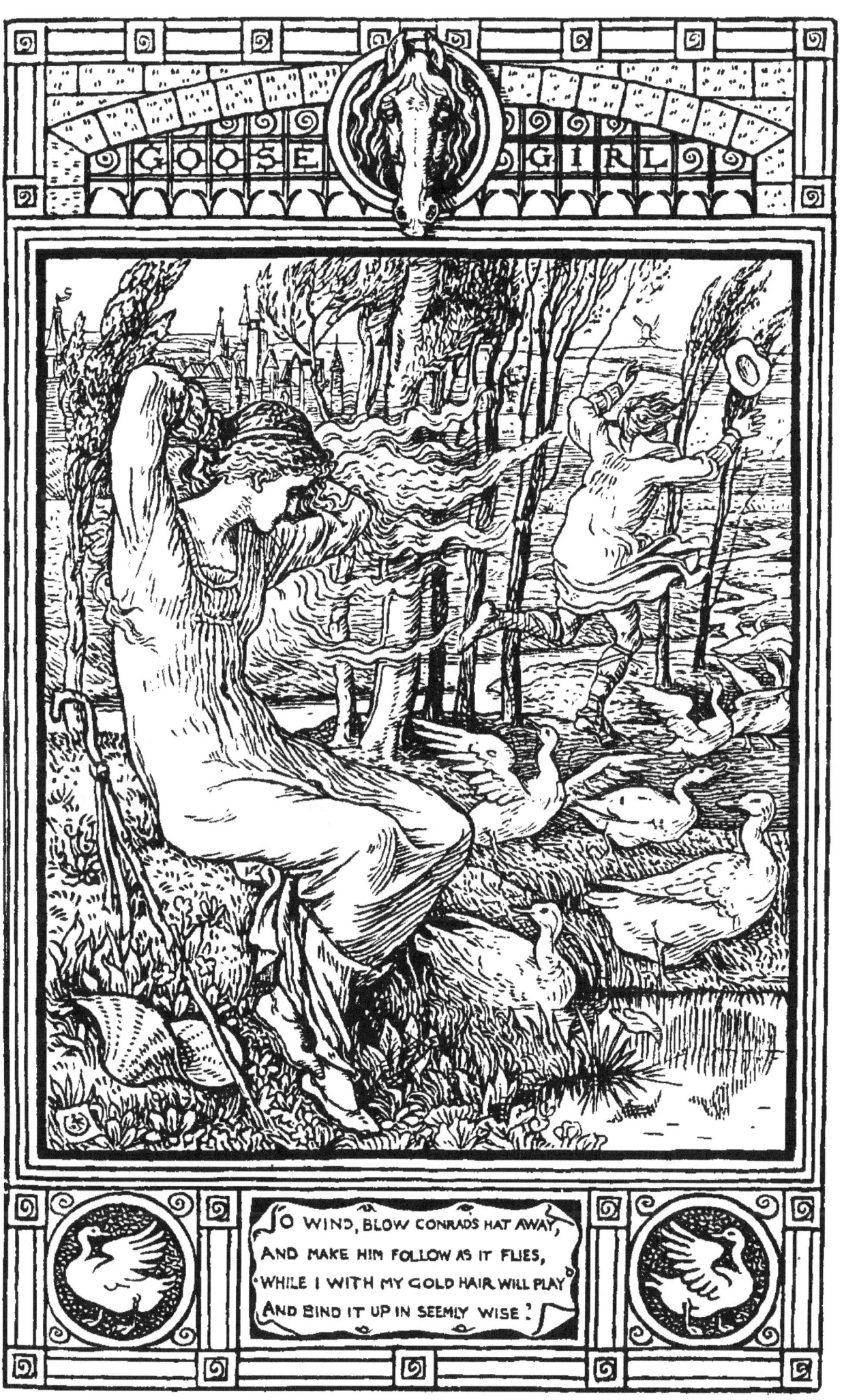

GOOSE GIRL

'O WIND, BLOW CONRADS HAT AWAY,
AND MAKE HIM FOLLOW AS IT FLIES,
WHILE I WITH MY GOLD HAIR WILL PLAY
AND BIND IT UP IN SEEMLY WISE.'

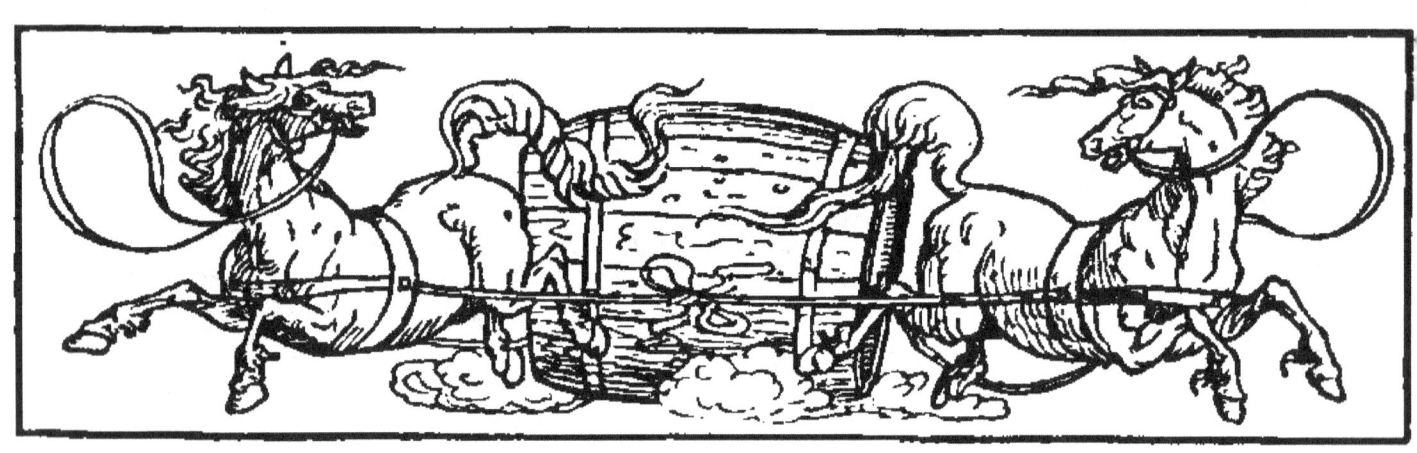

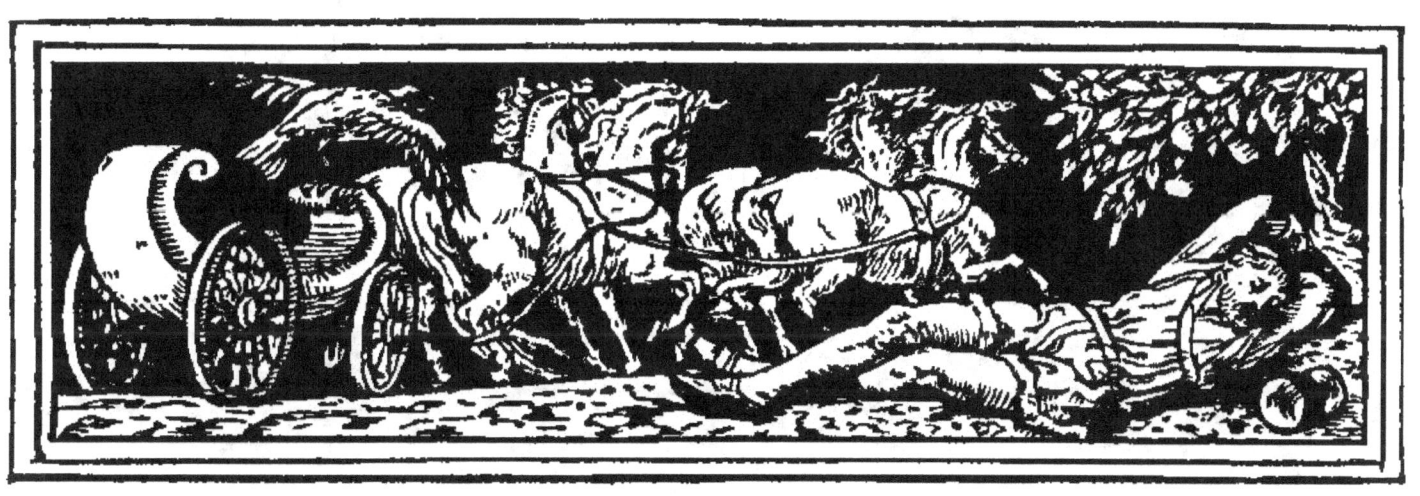

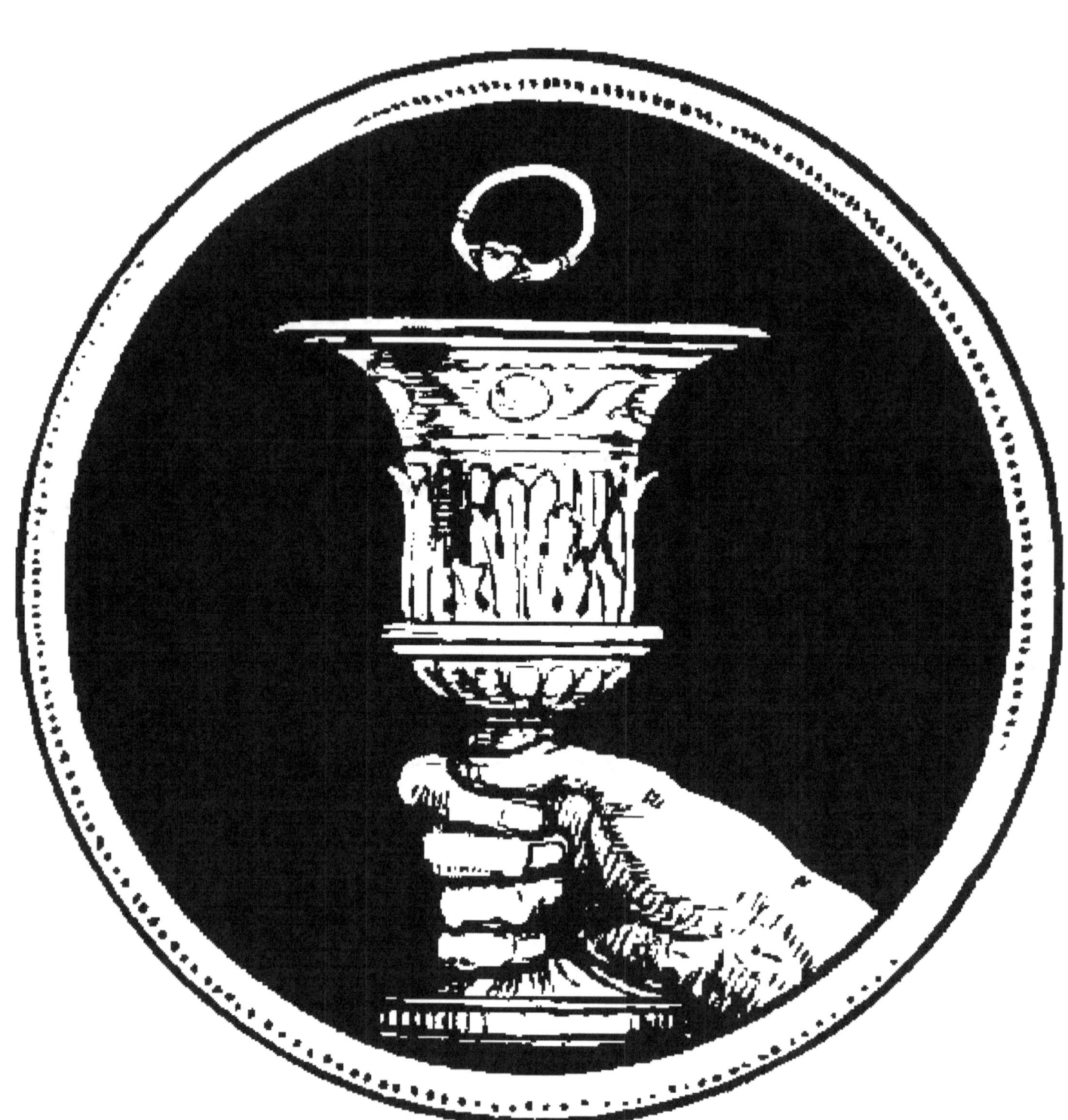

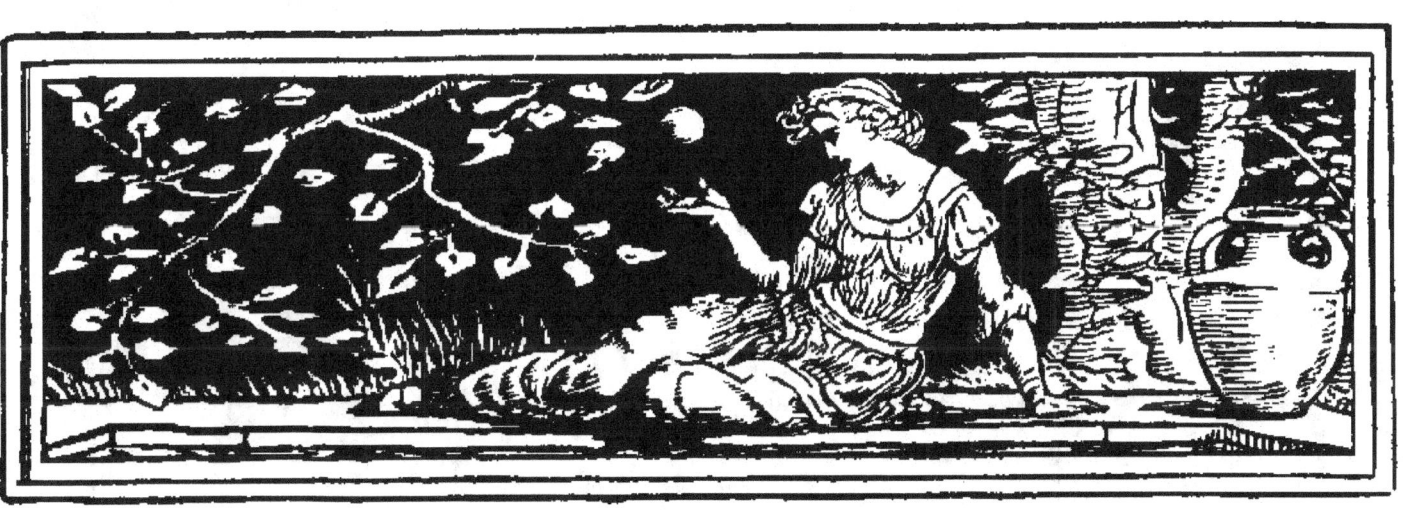

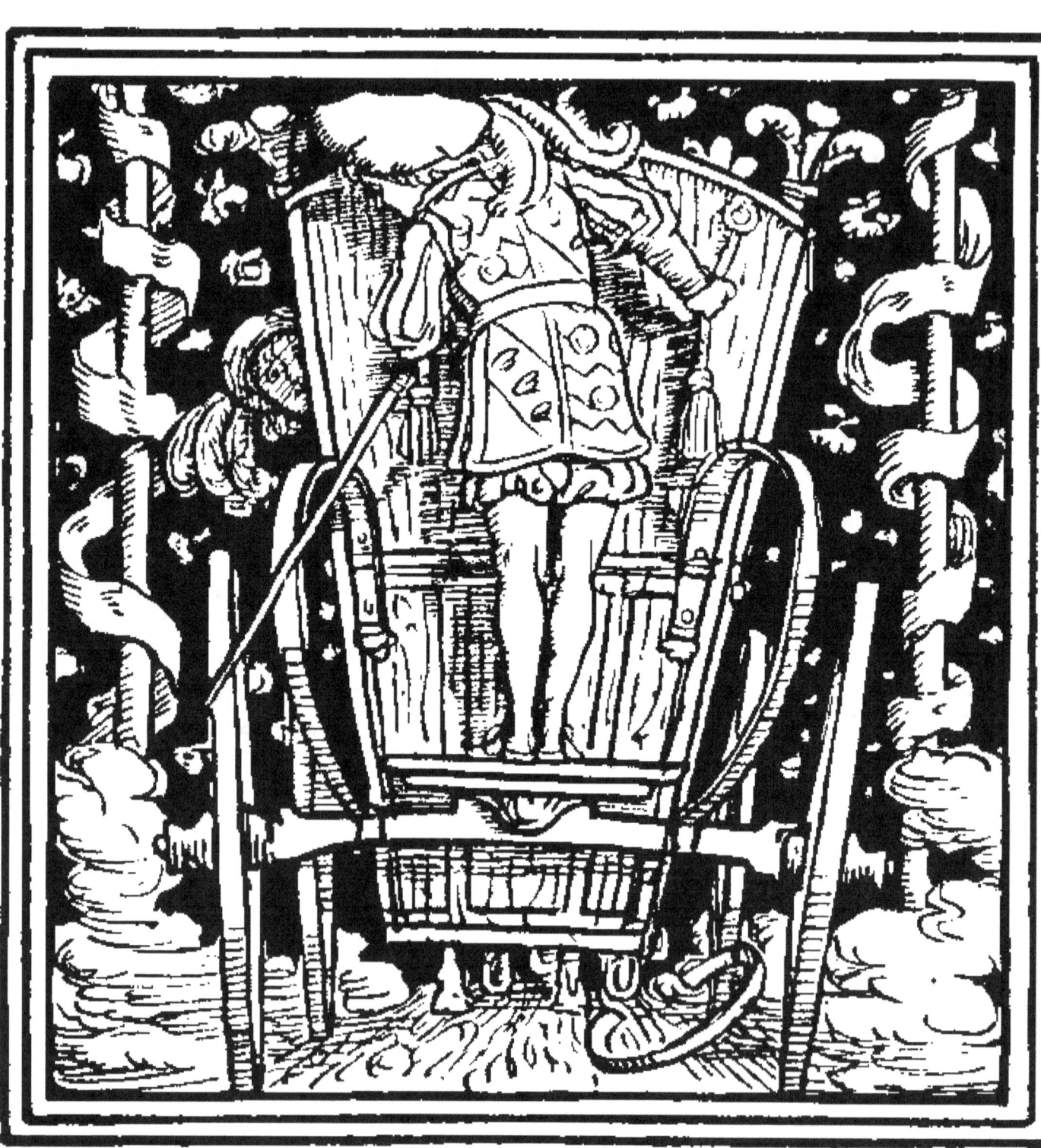

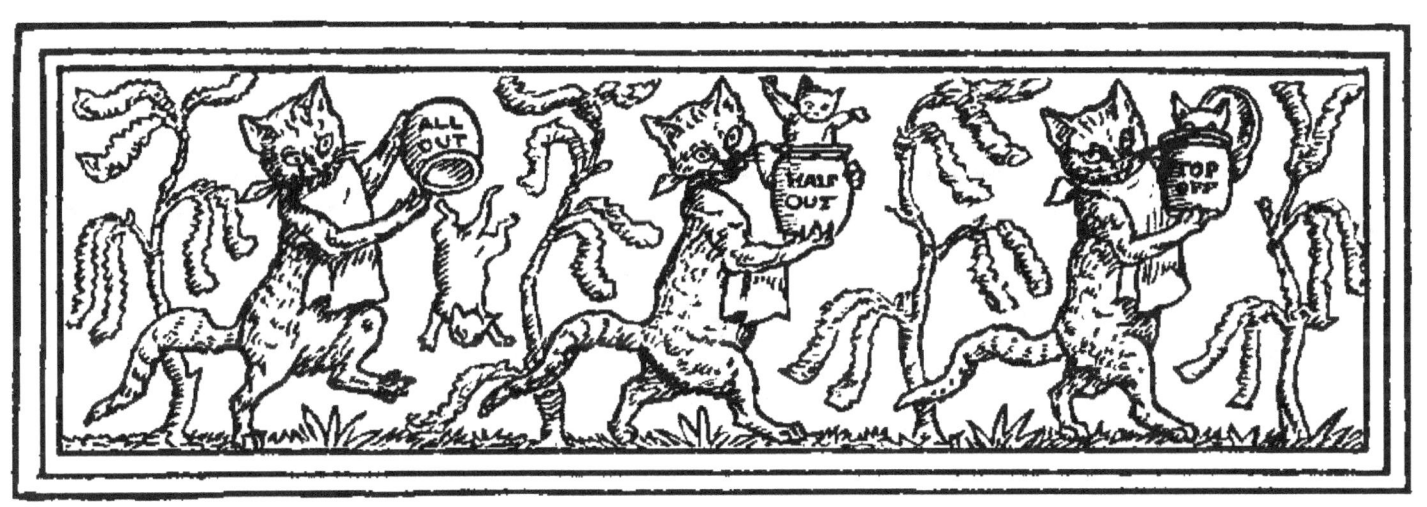

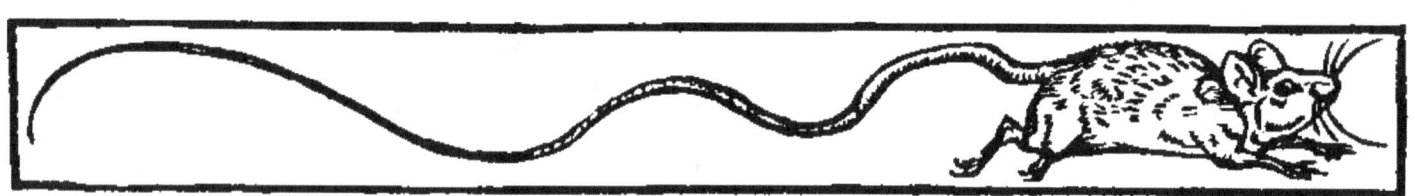

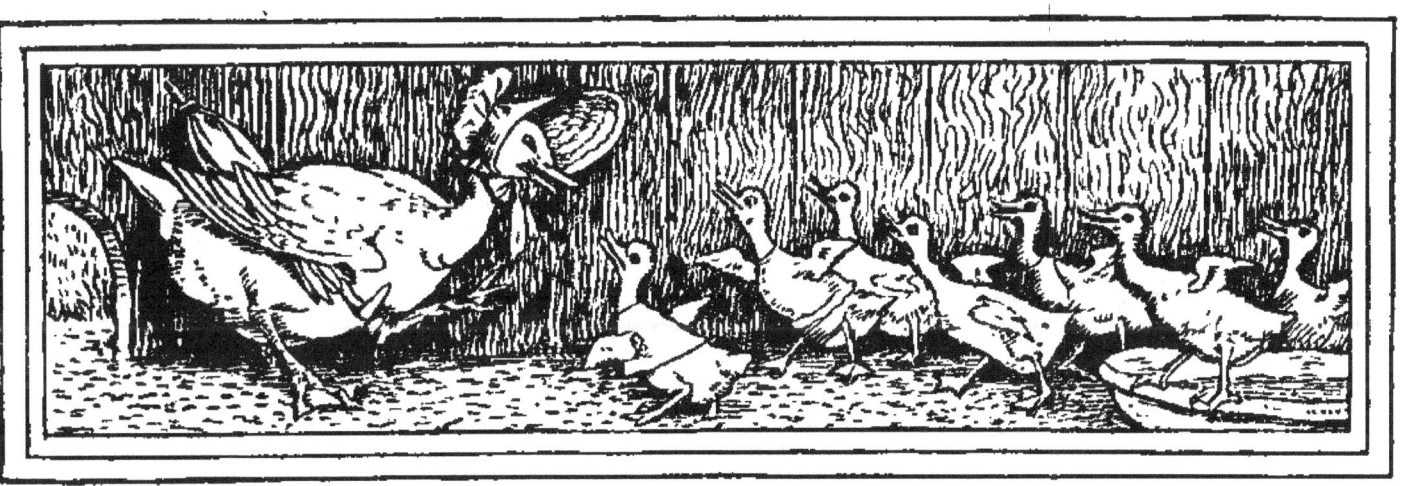

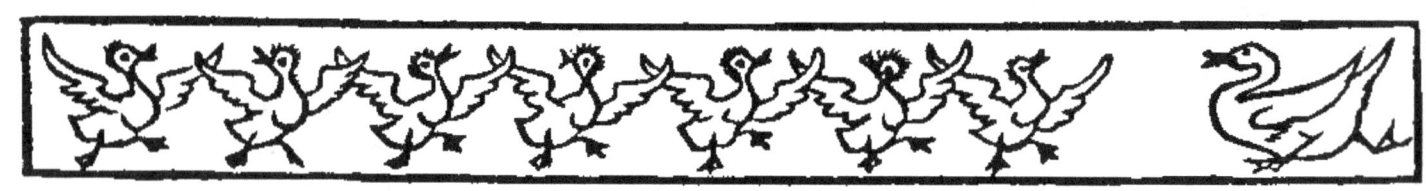

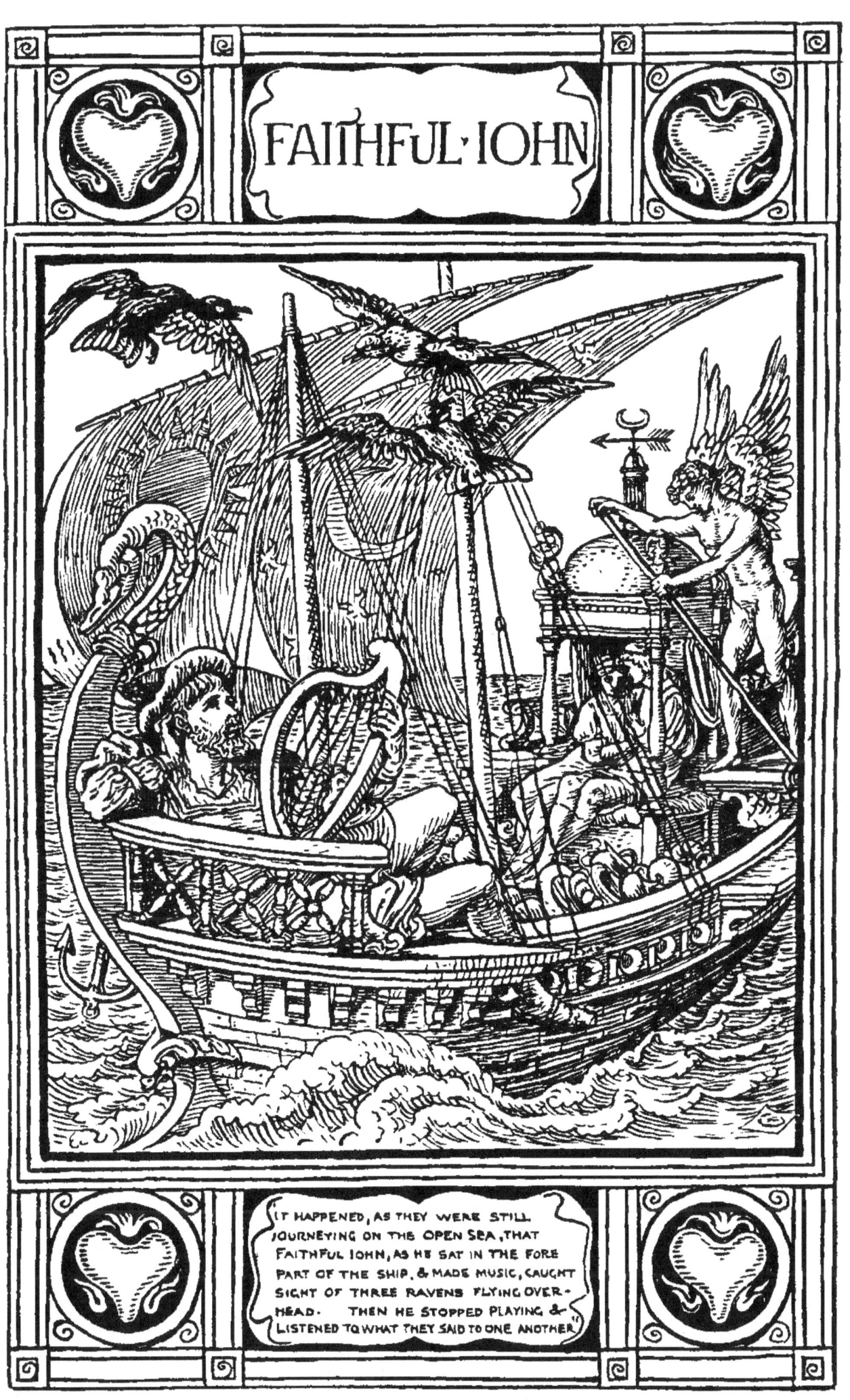

FAITHFUL·IOHN

IT HAPPENED, AS THEY WERE STILL
JOURNEYING ON THE OPEN SEA, THAT
FAITHFUL IOHN, AS HE SAT IN THE FORE
PART OF THE SHIP, & MADE MUSIC, CAUGHT
SIGHT OF THREE RAVENS FLYING OVER-
HEAD.   THEN HE STOPPED PLAYING &
LISTENED TO WHAT THEY SAID TO ONE ANOTHER

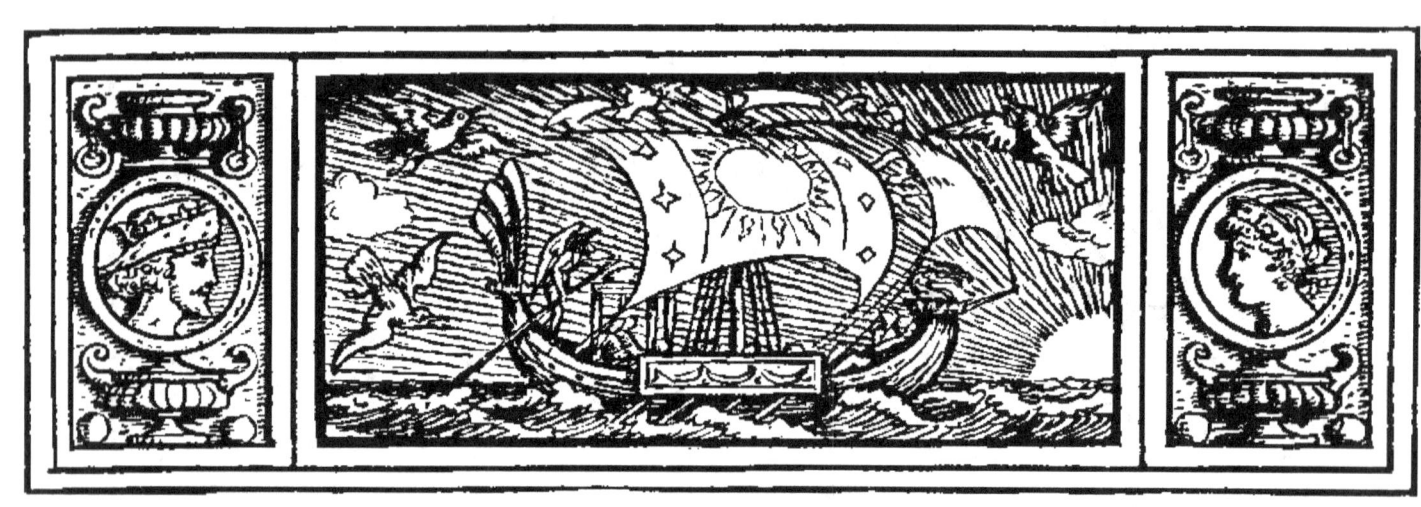

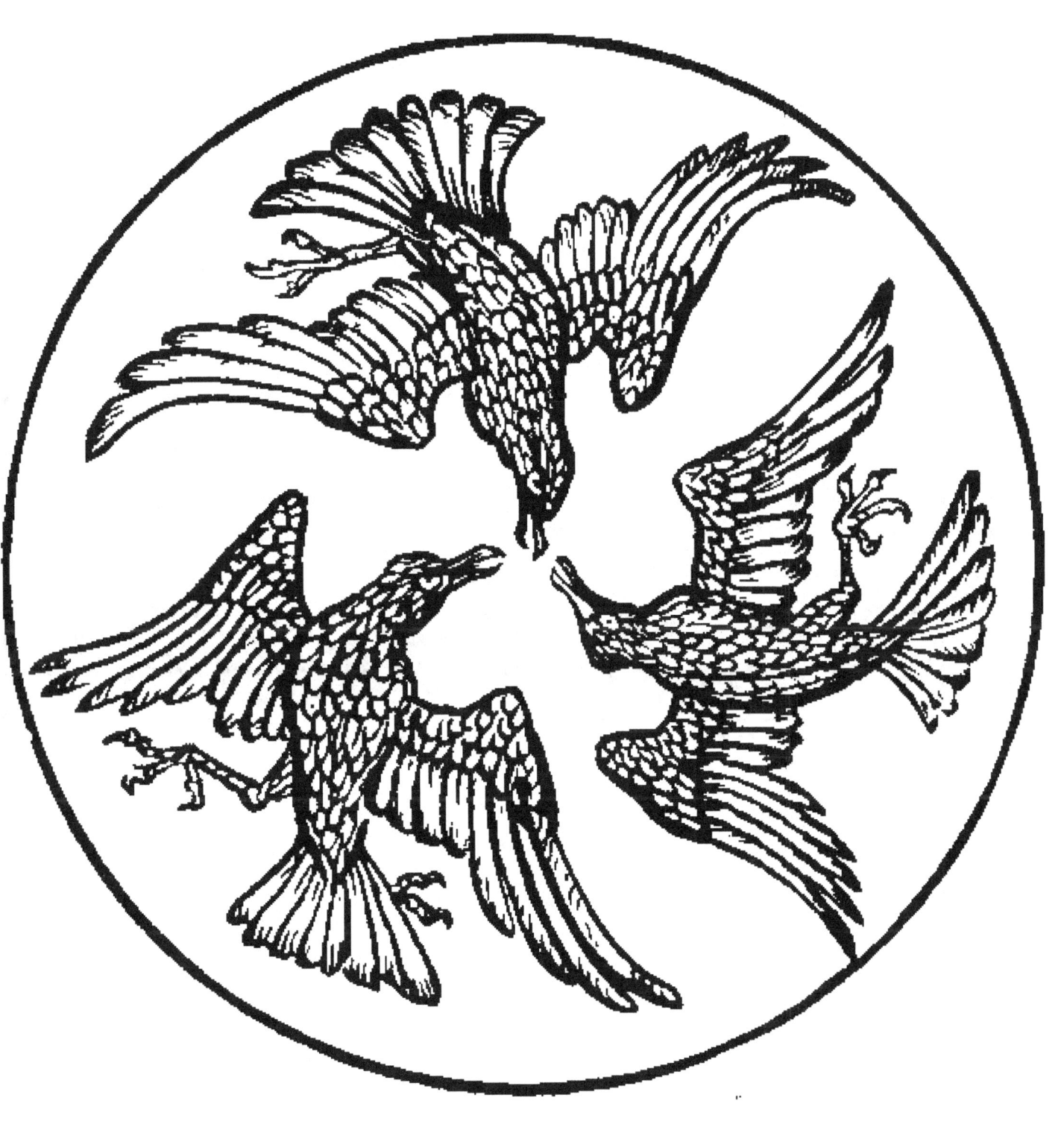

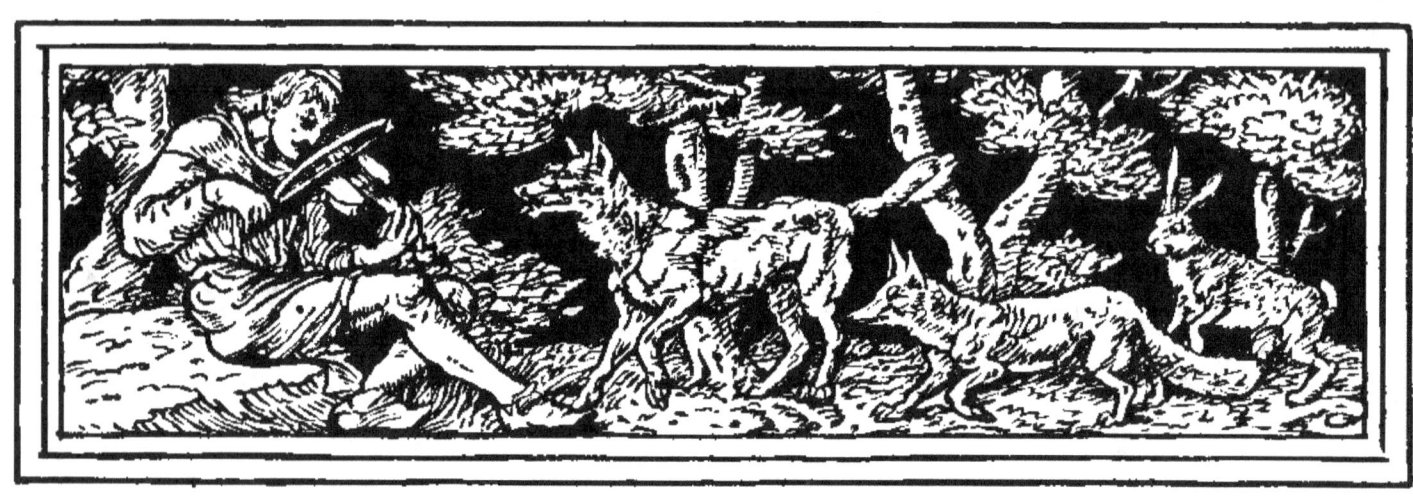

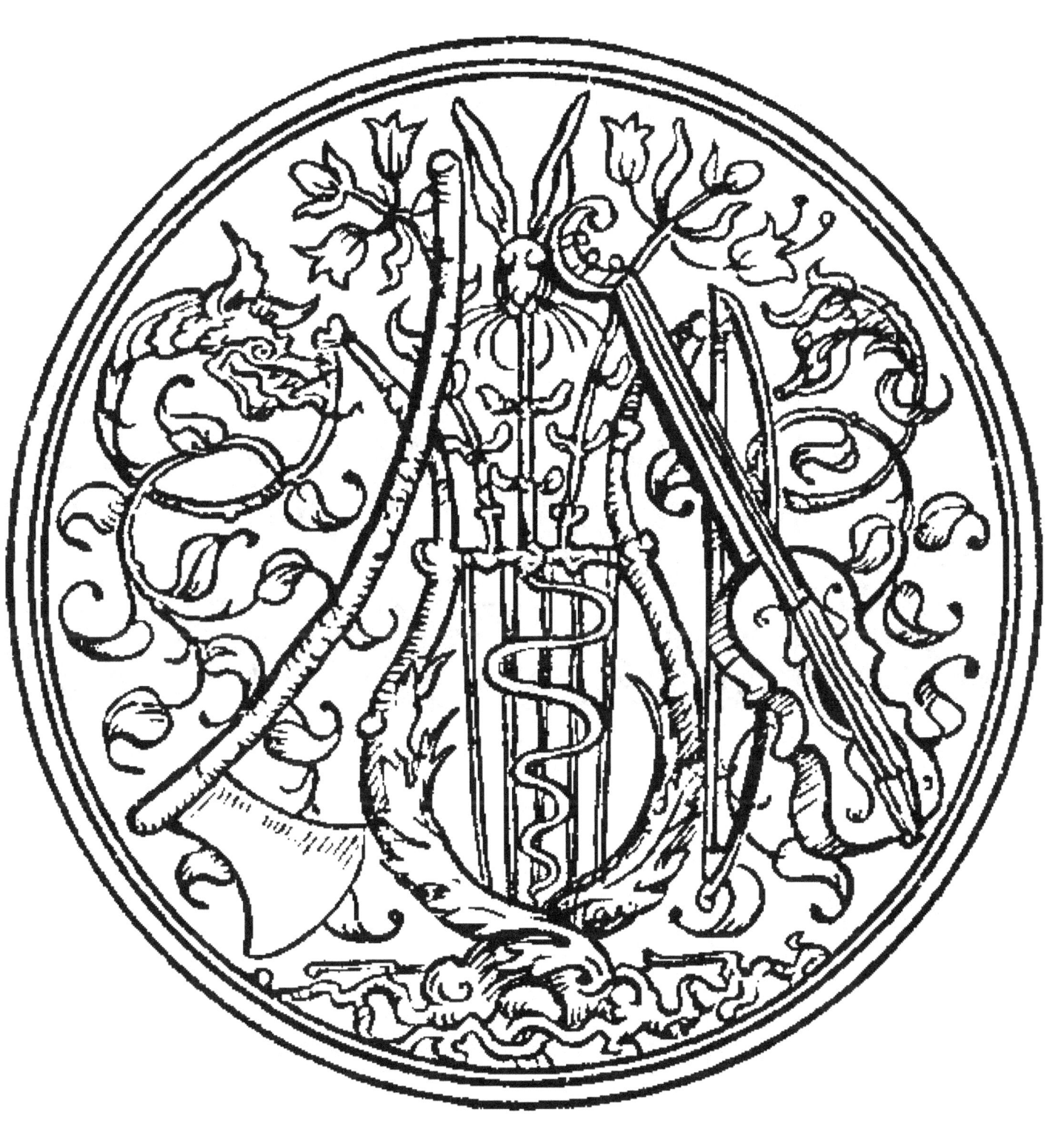

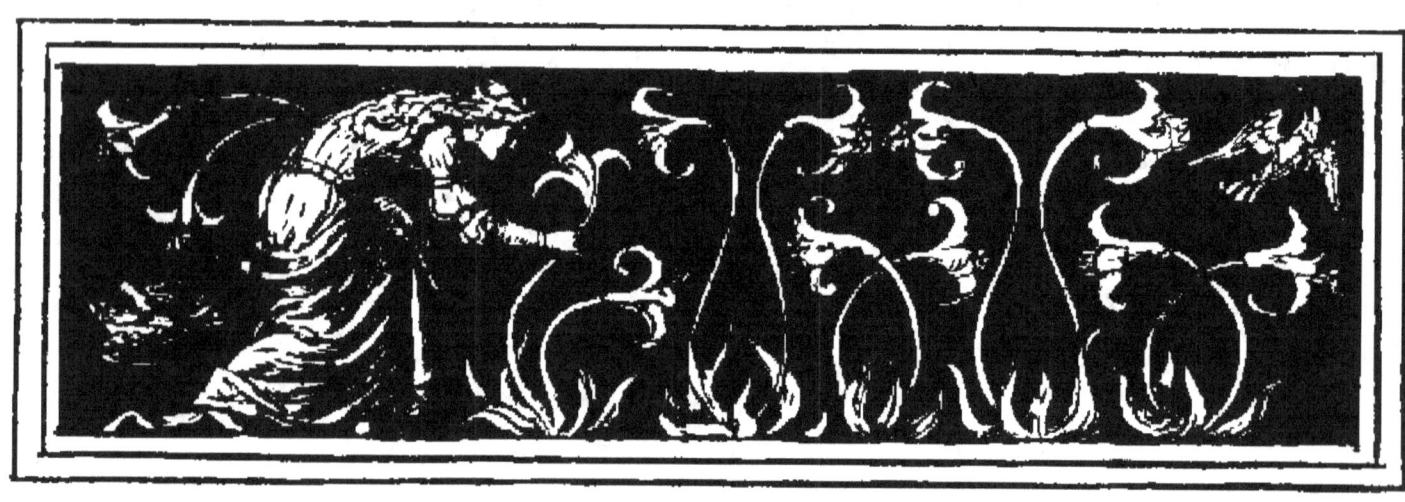

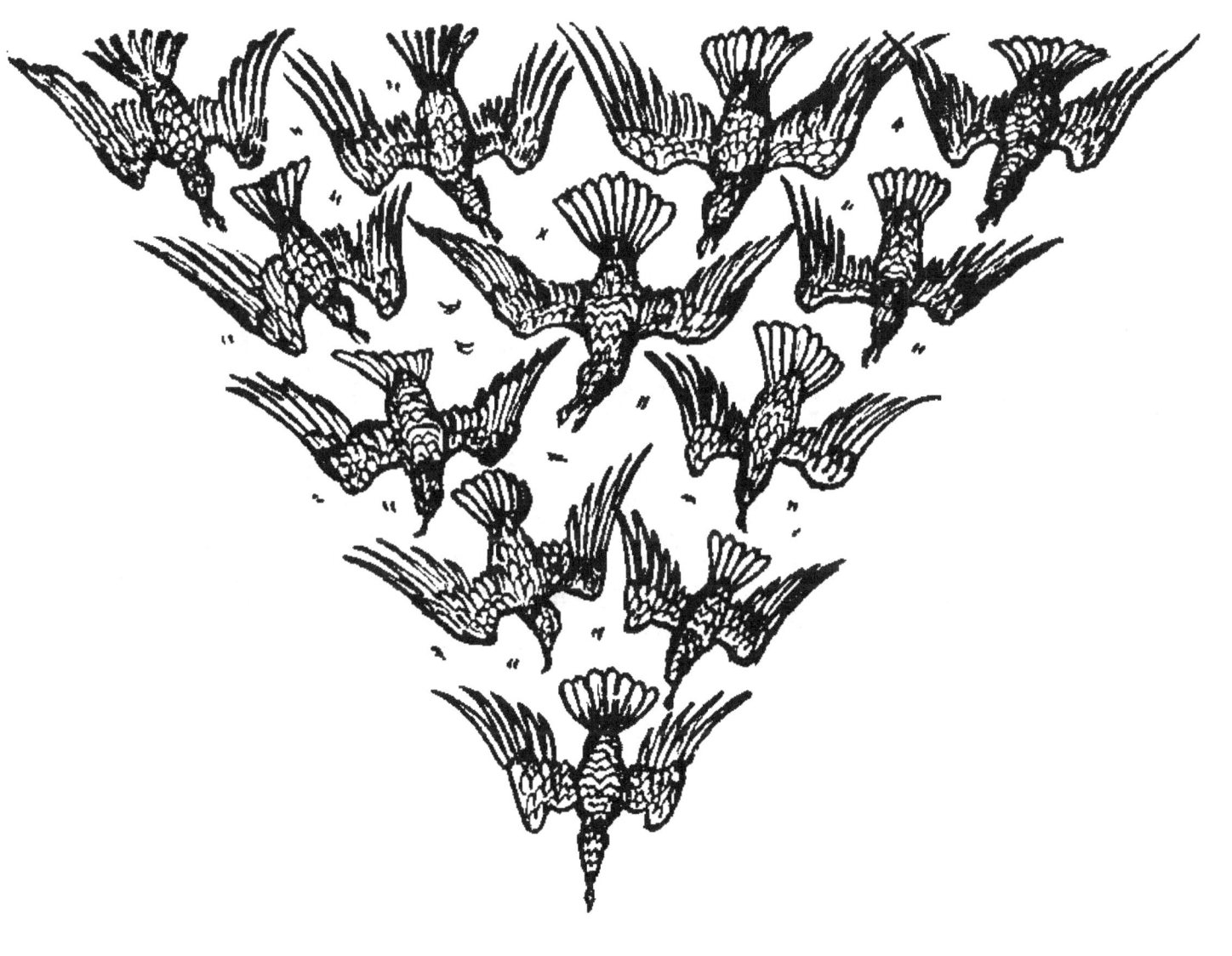

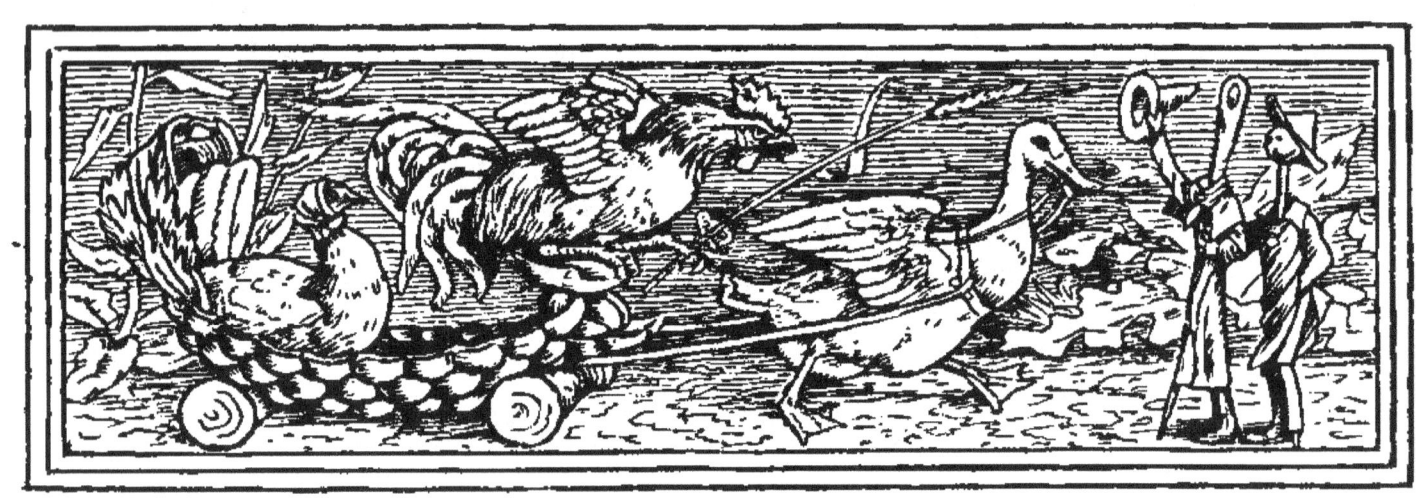

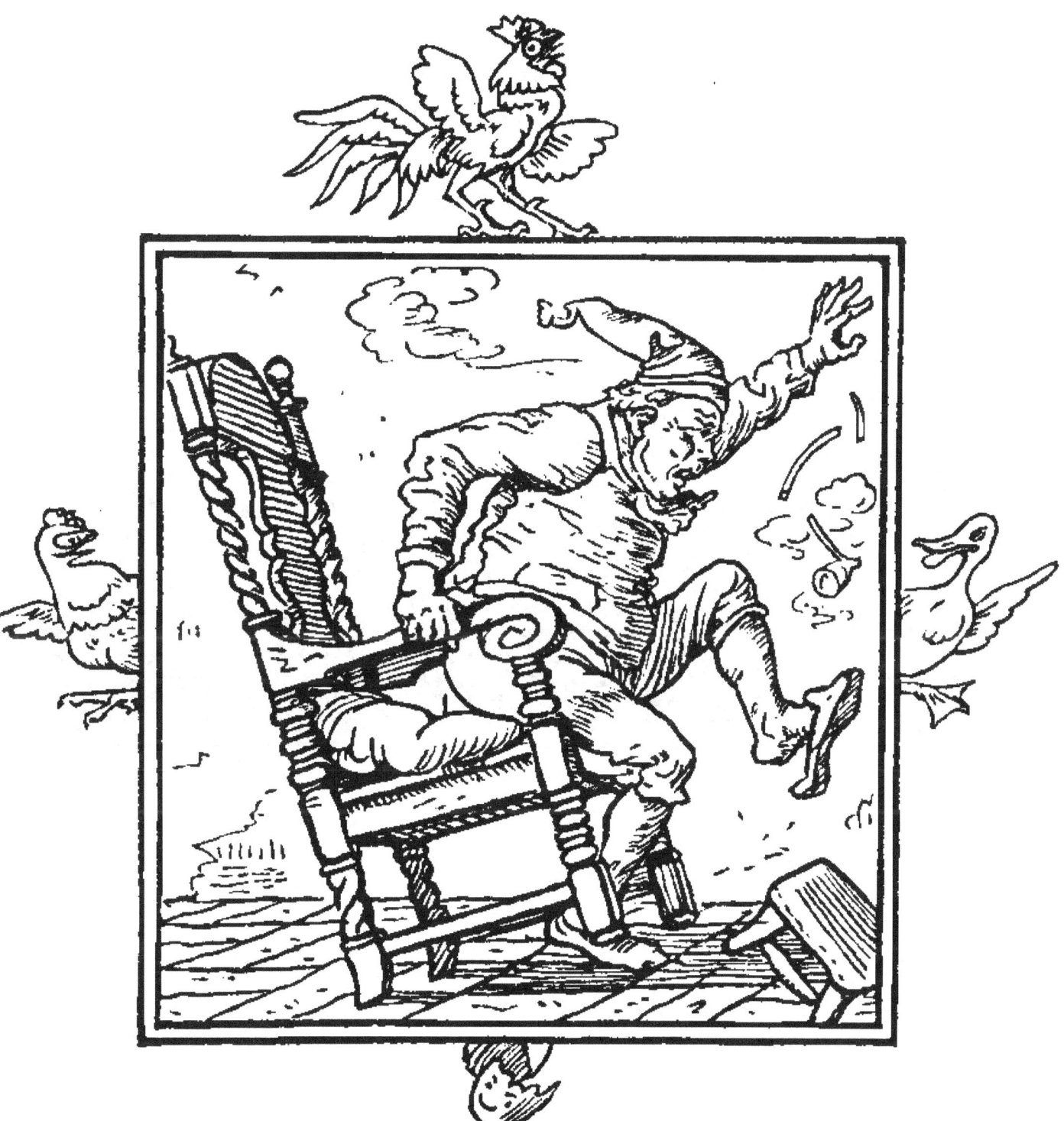

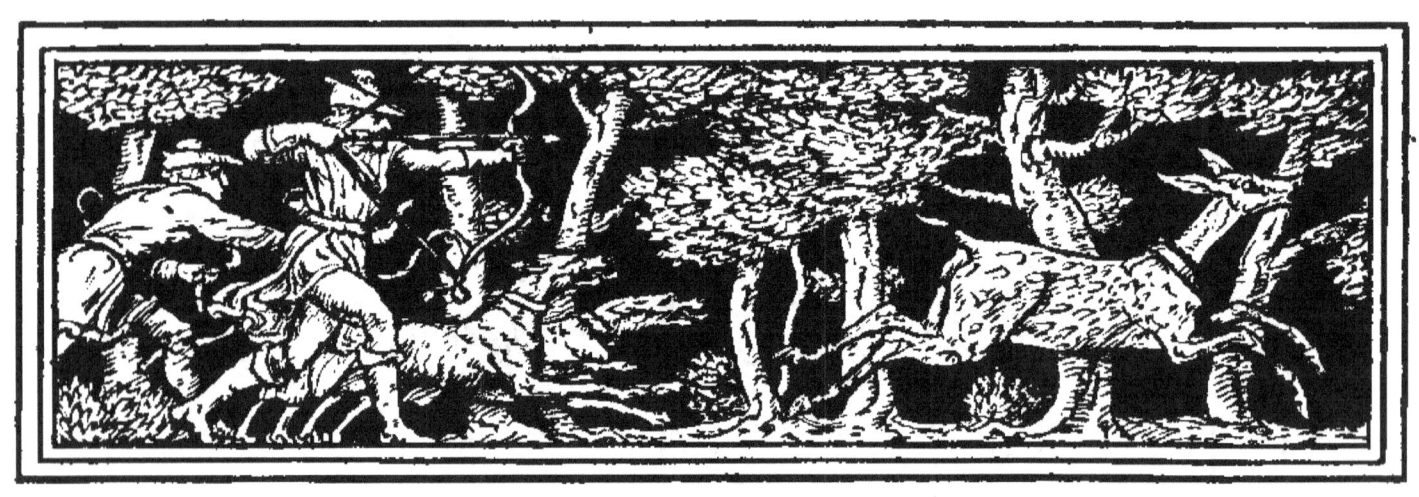

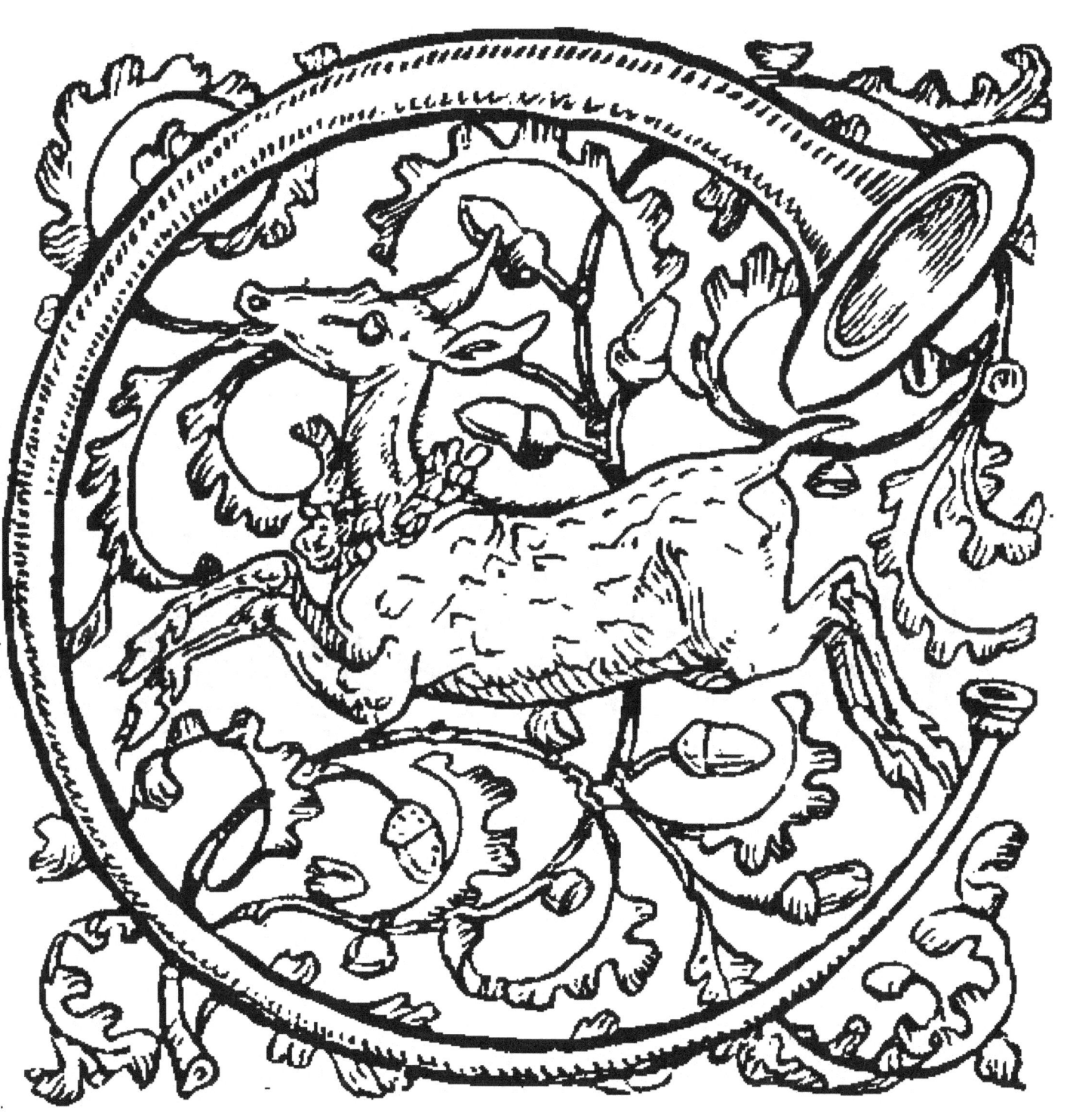

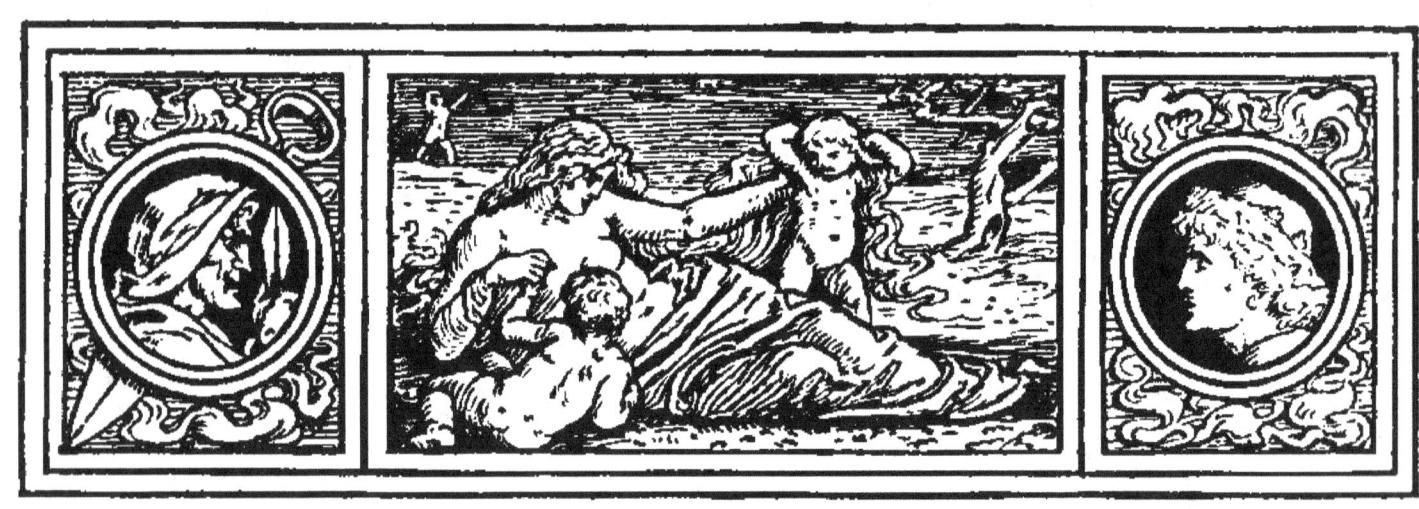

RAPUNZEL

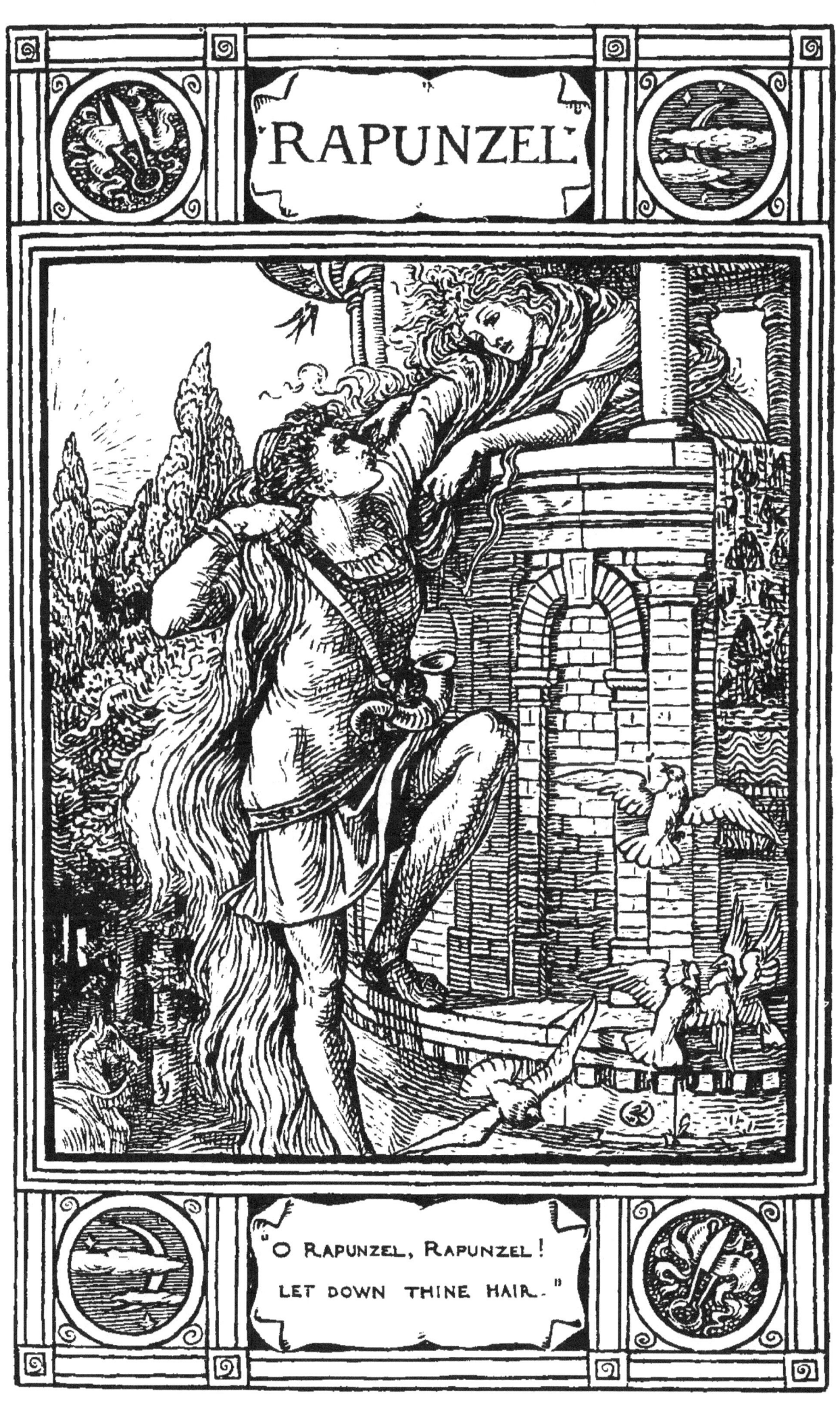

"O RAPUNZEL, RAPUNZEL!
LET DOWN THINE HAIR."

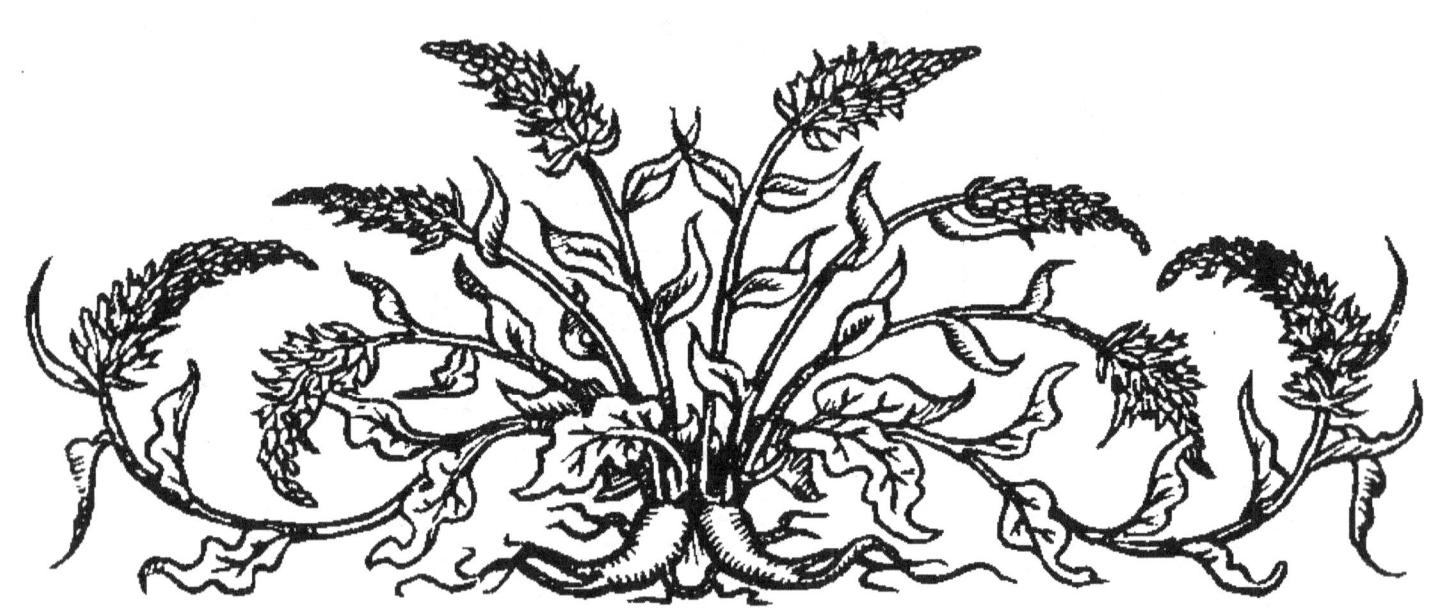

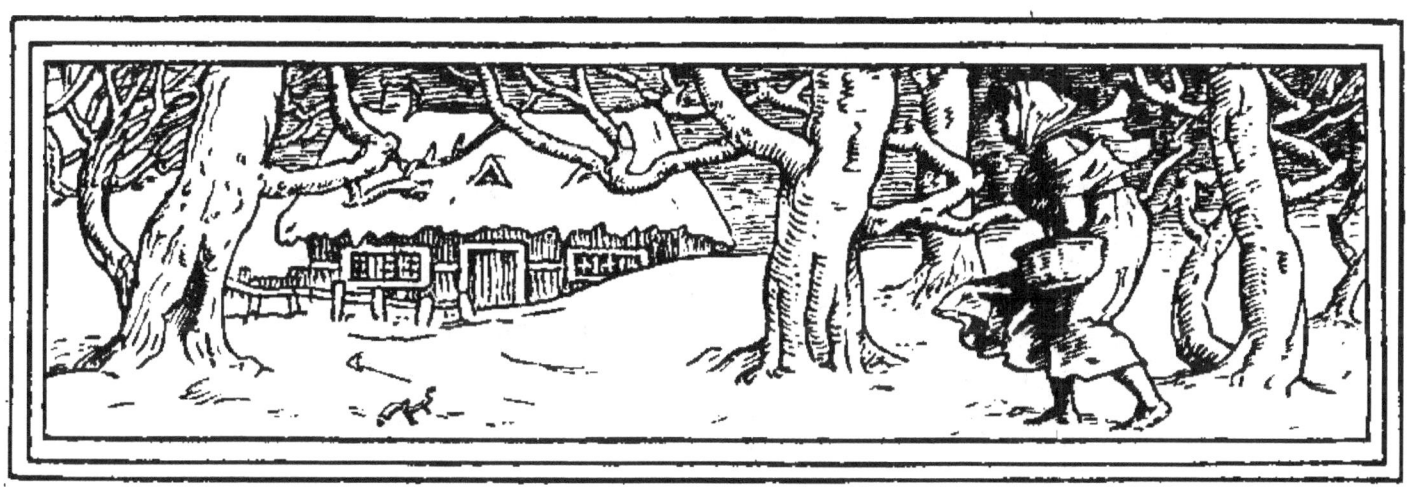

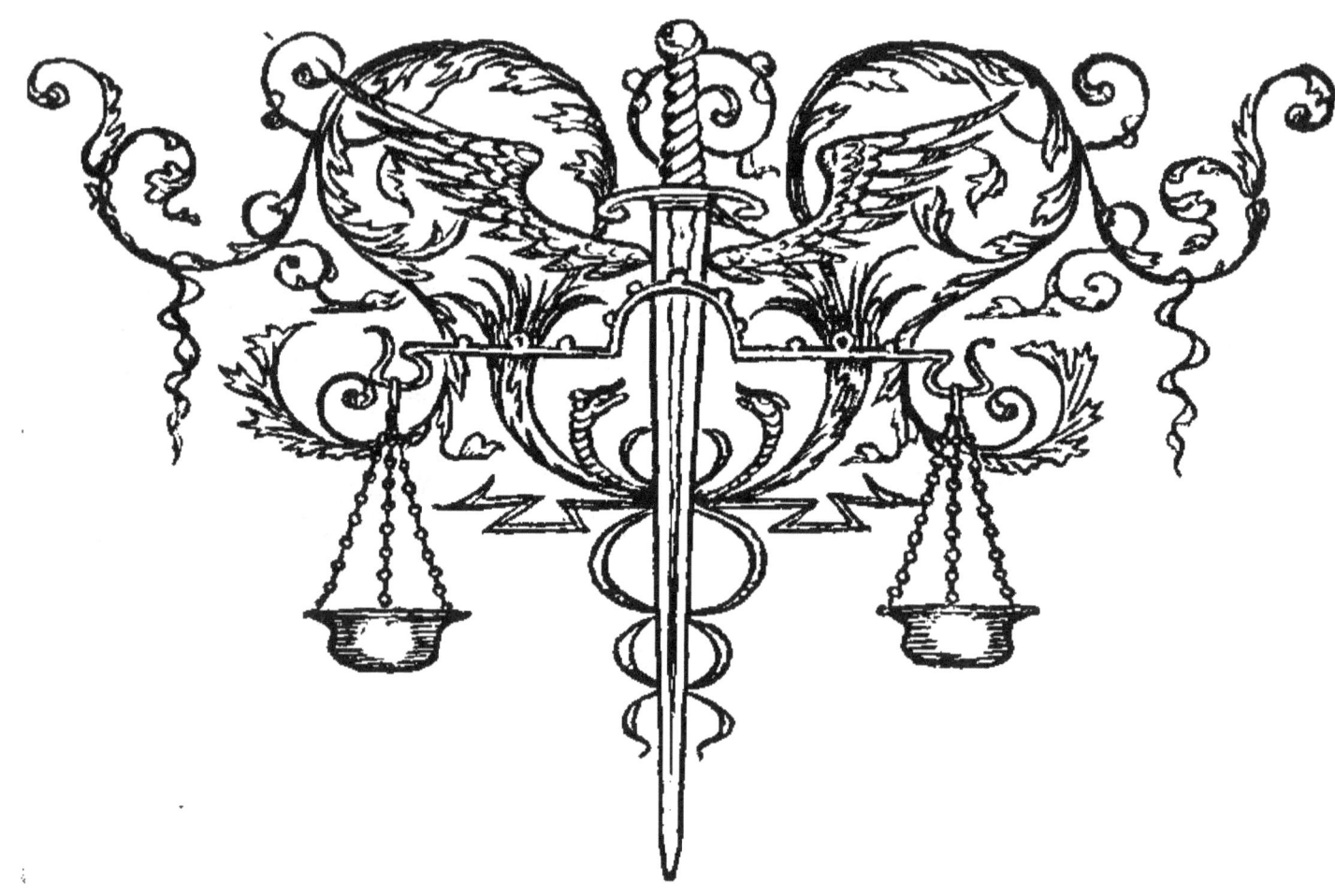

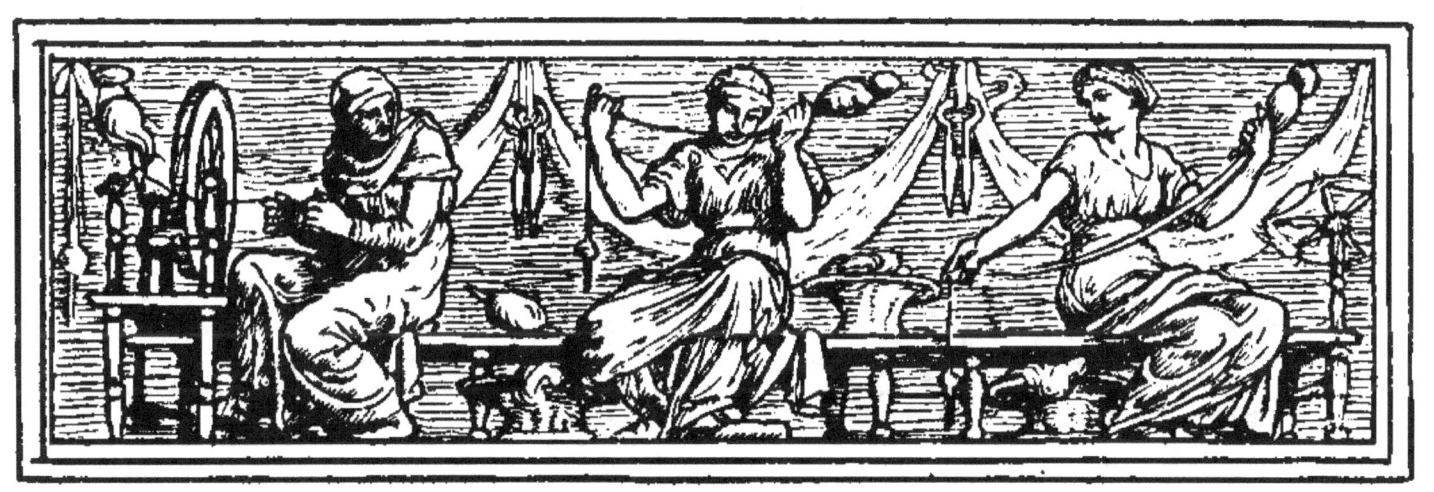

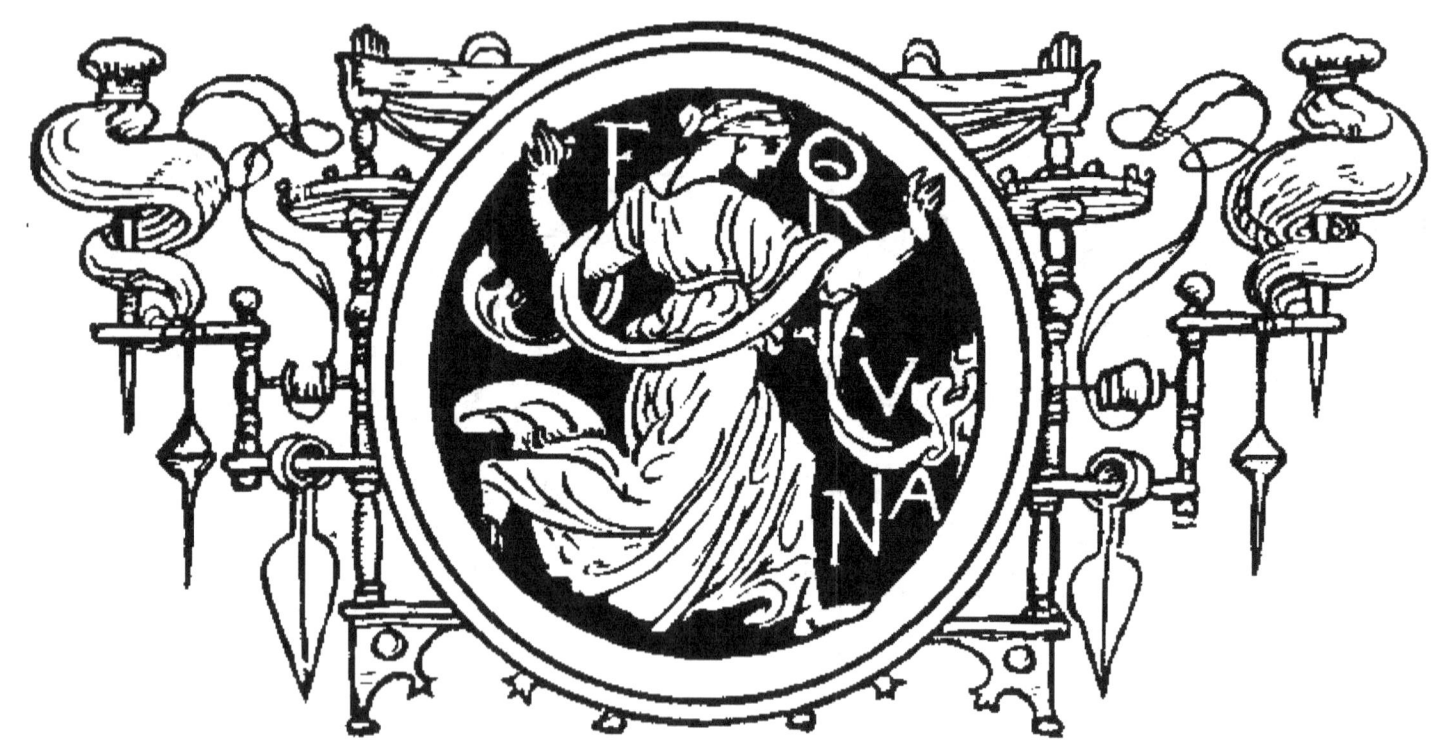

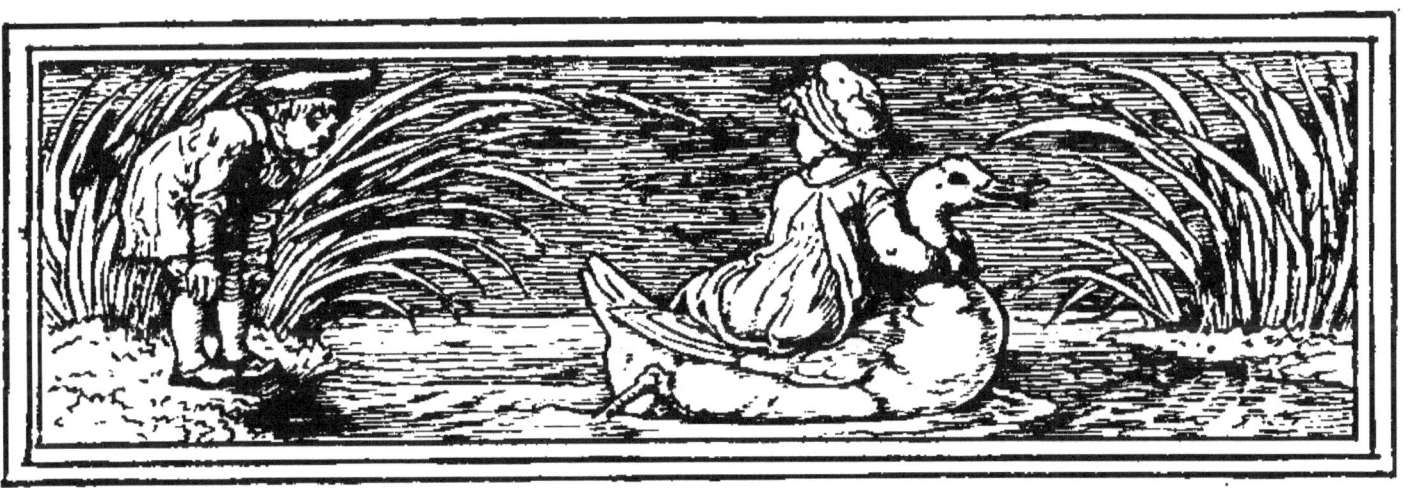

Sing every one,
My story is done,
And look! round the house
There runs a little mouse,
He that can catch her before she scampers in,
May make himself a very very large fur-cap
out of her skin.

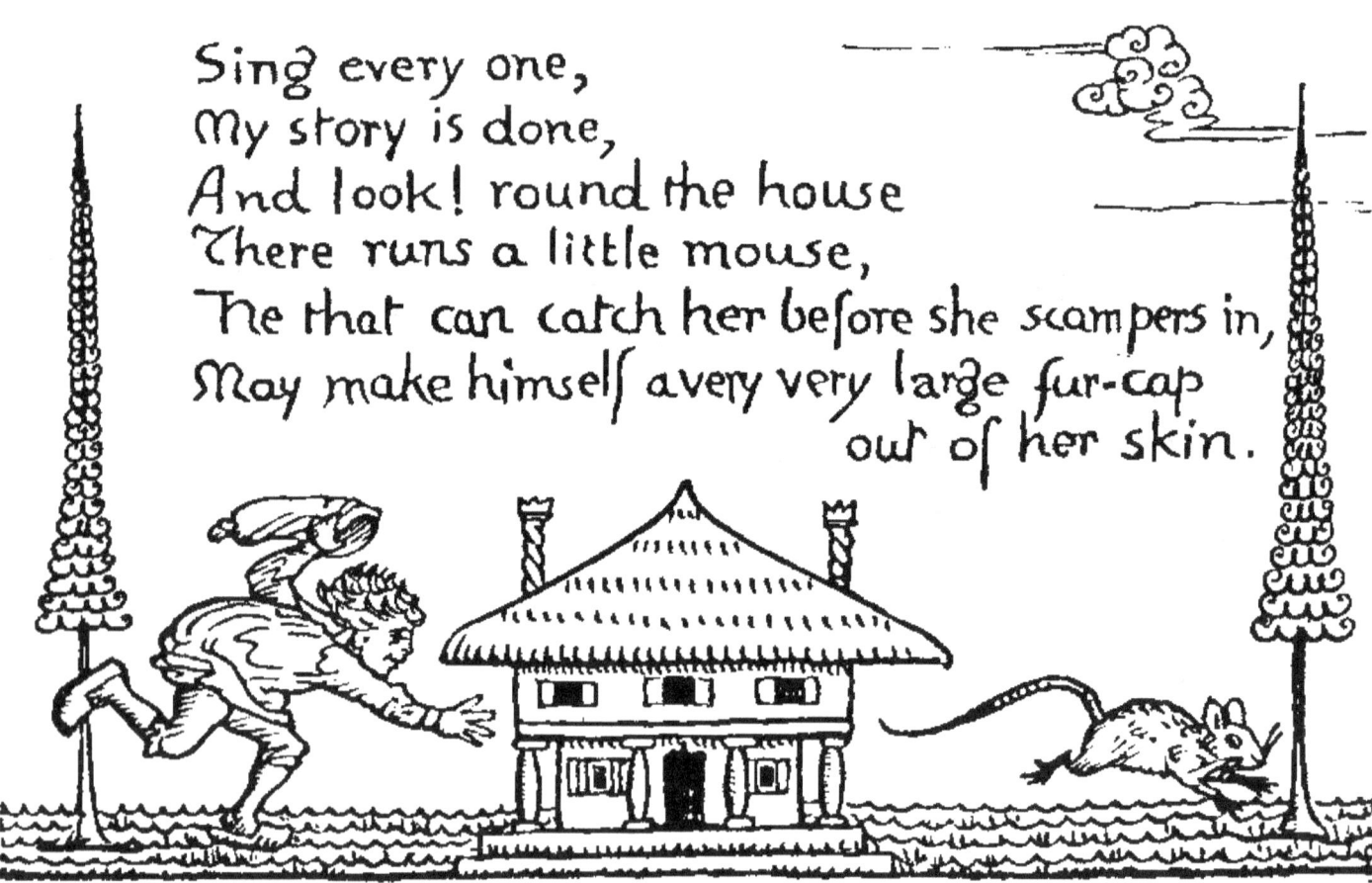

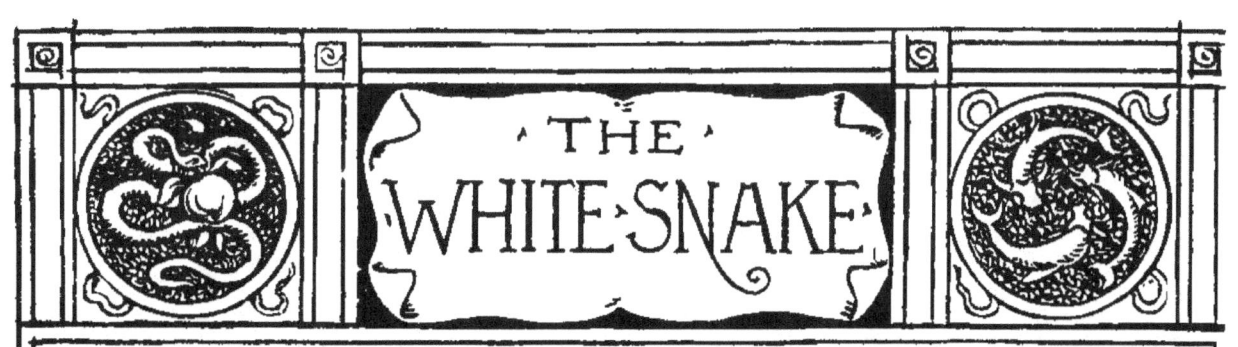

· THE · WHITE·SNAKE

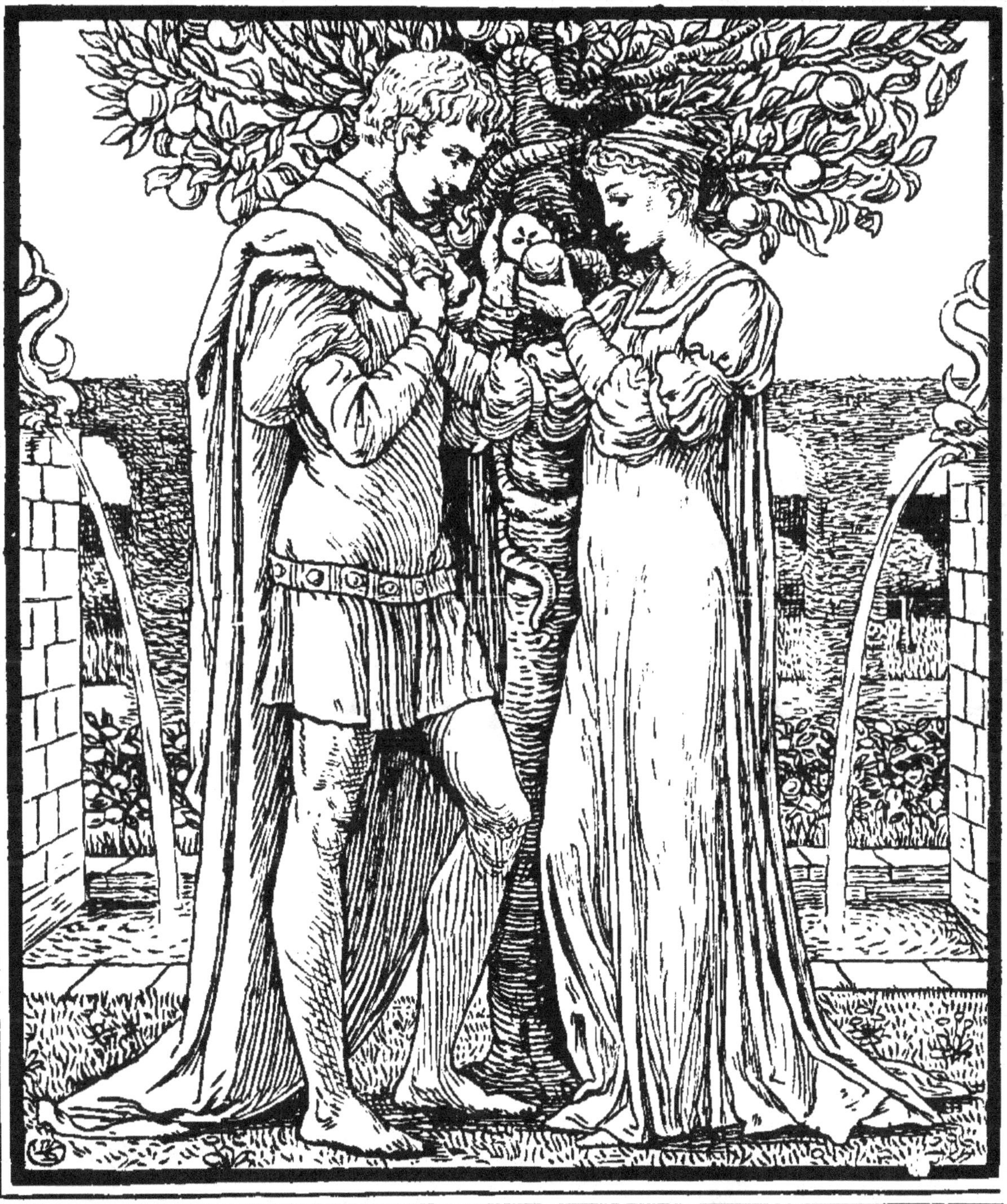

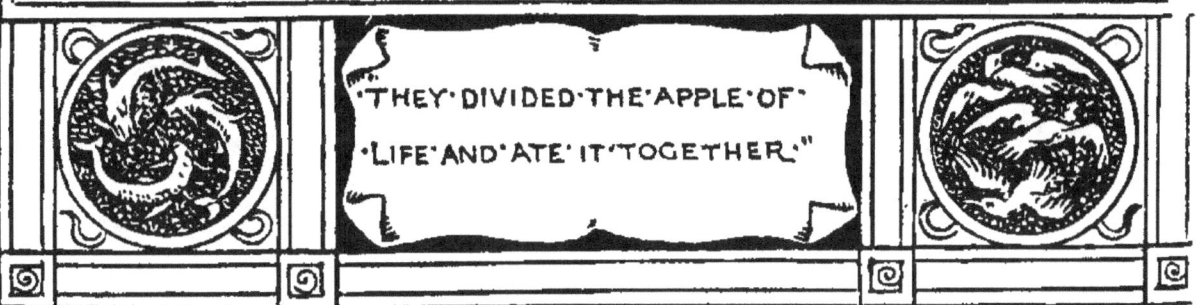

"·THEY·DIVIDED·THE·APPLE·OF·
·LIFE·AND·ATE·IT·TOGETHER·"

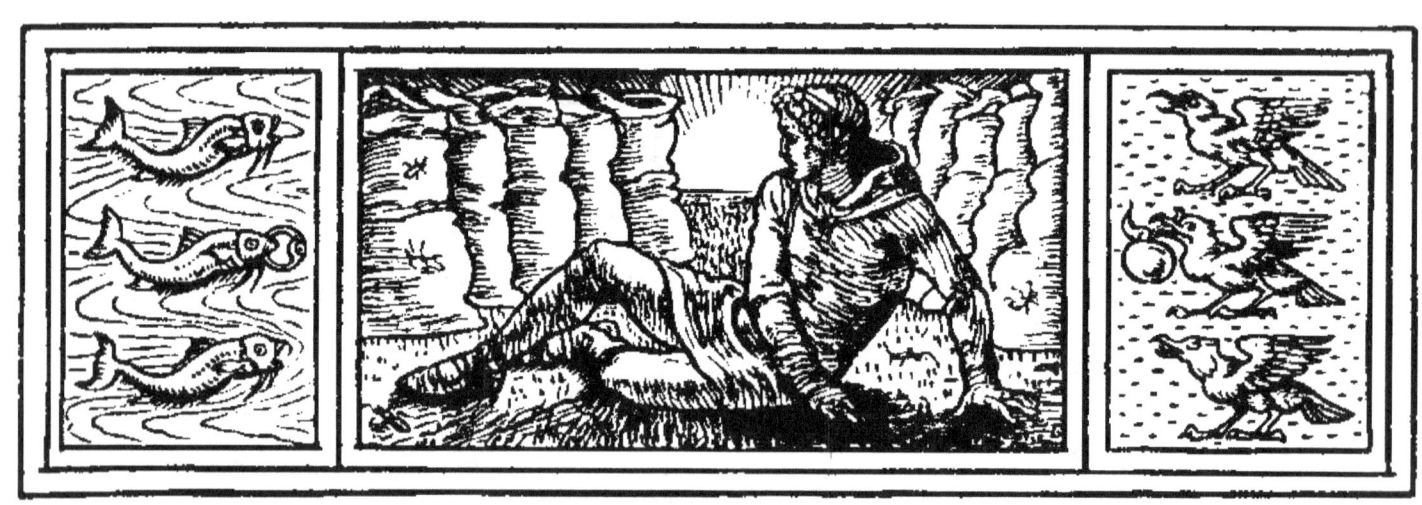

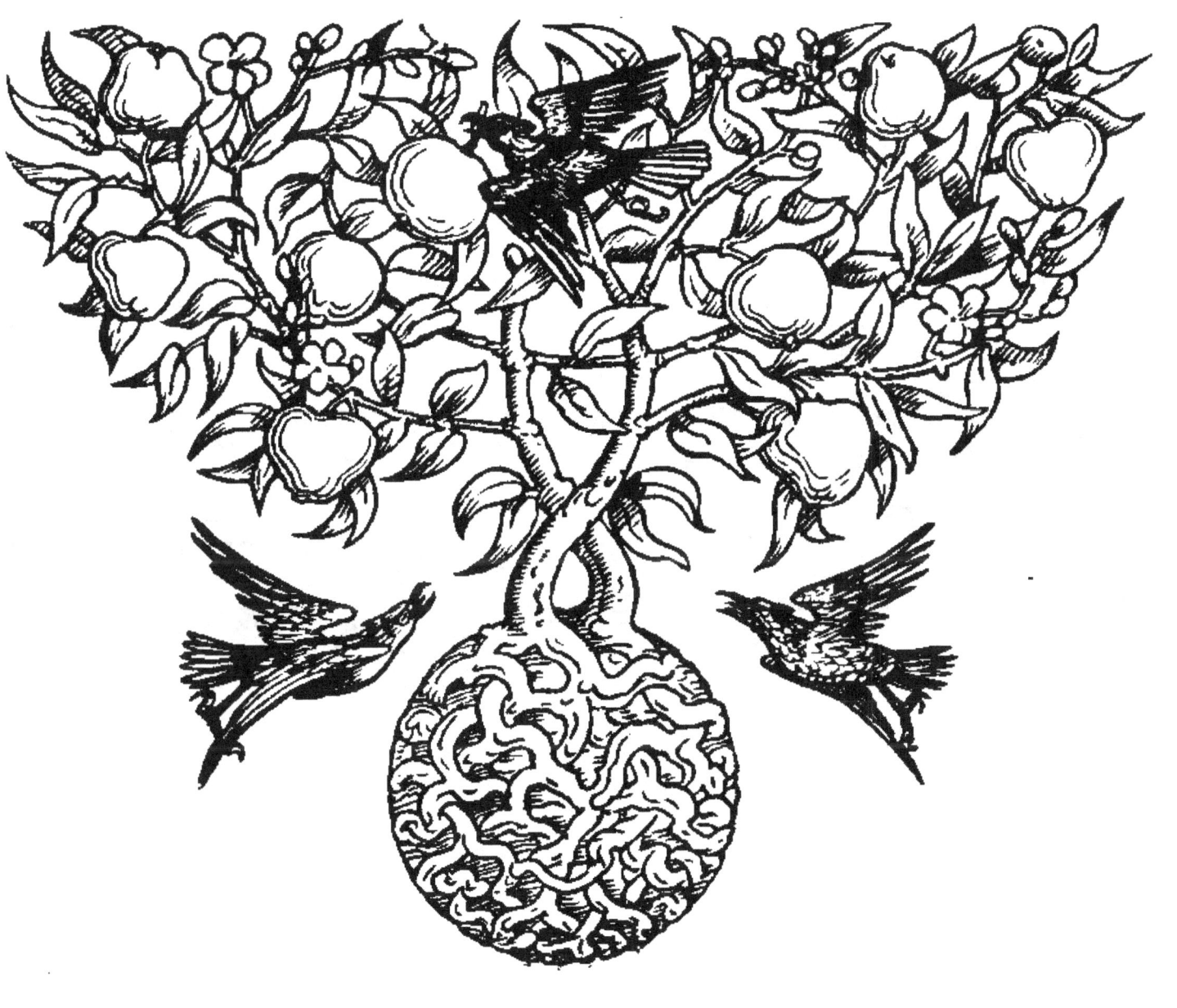

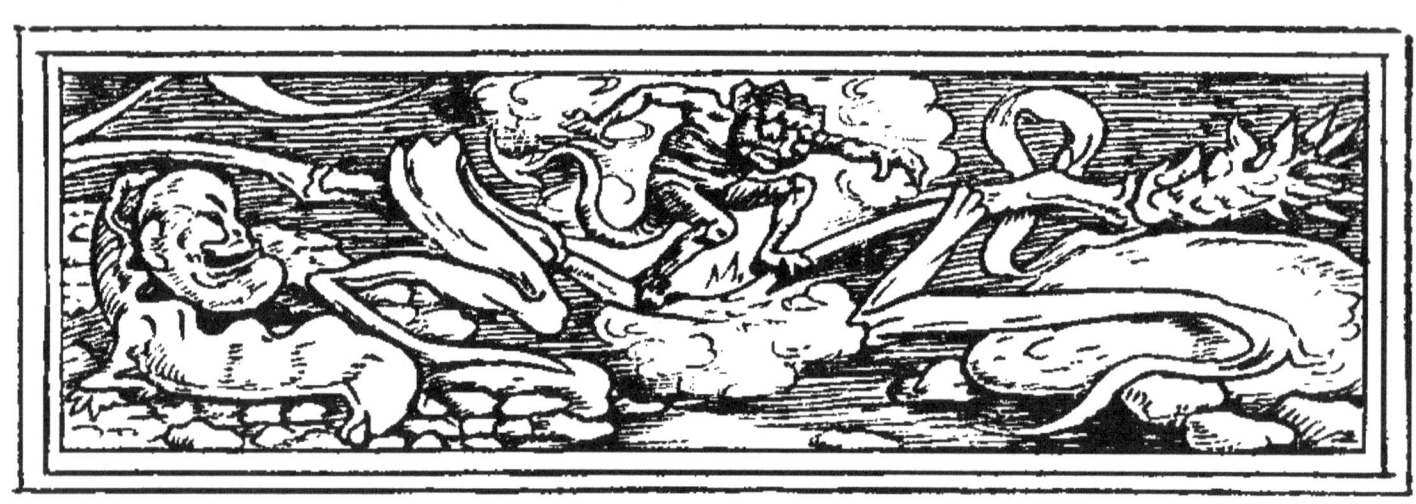

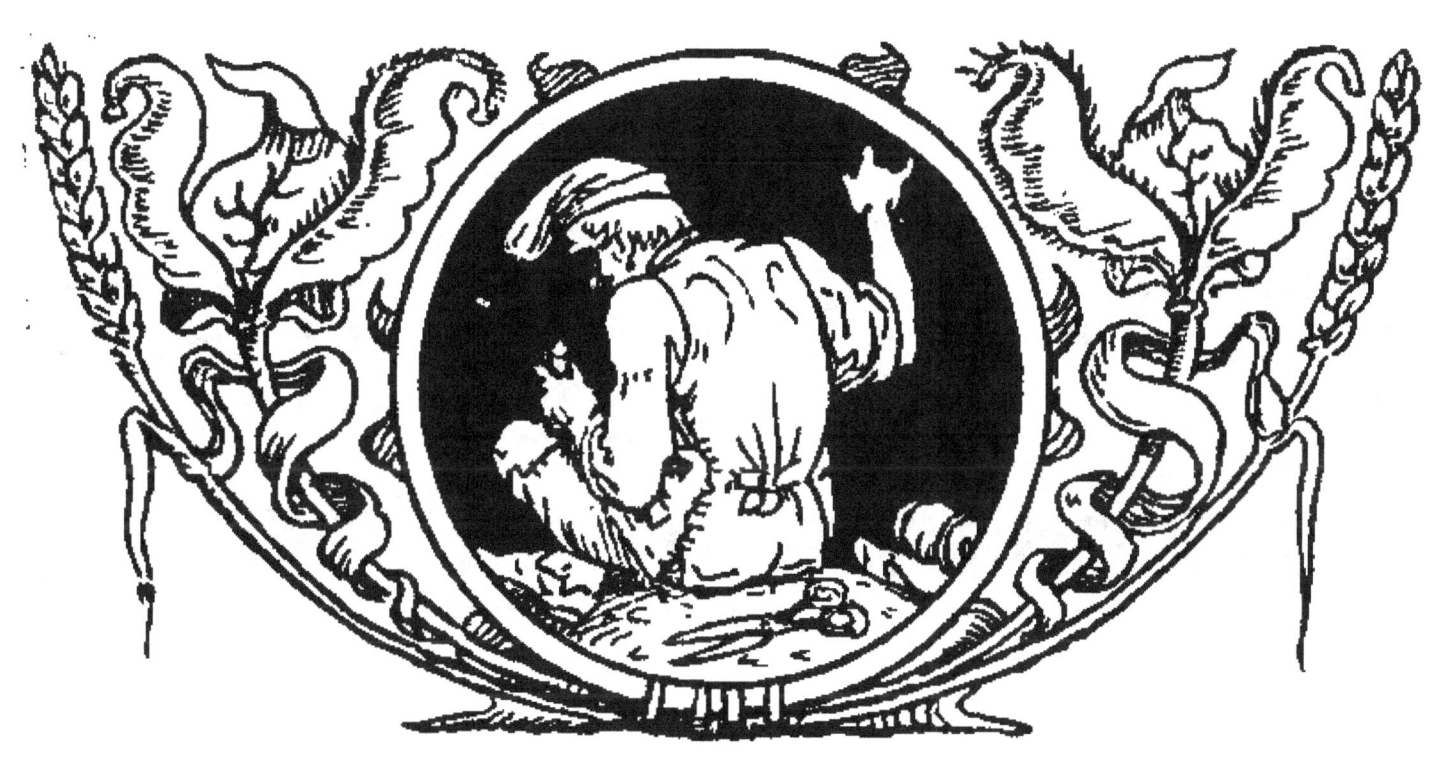

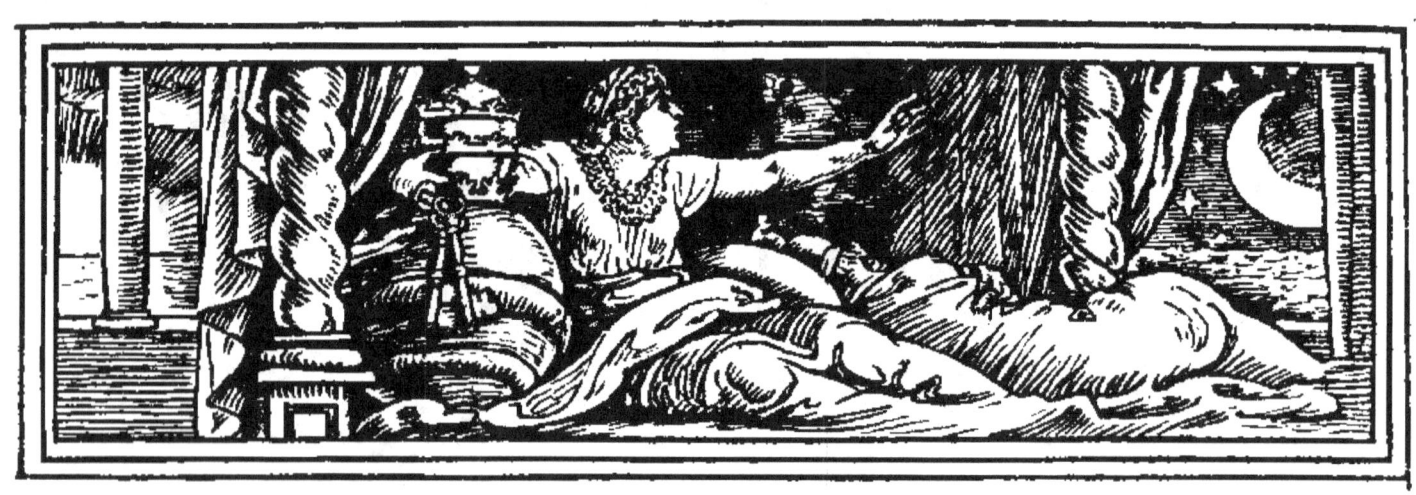

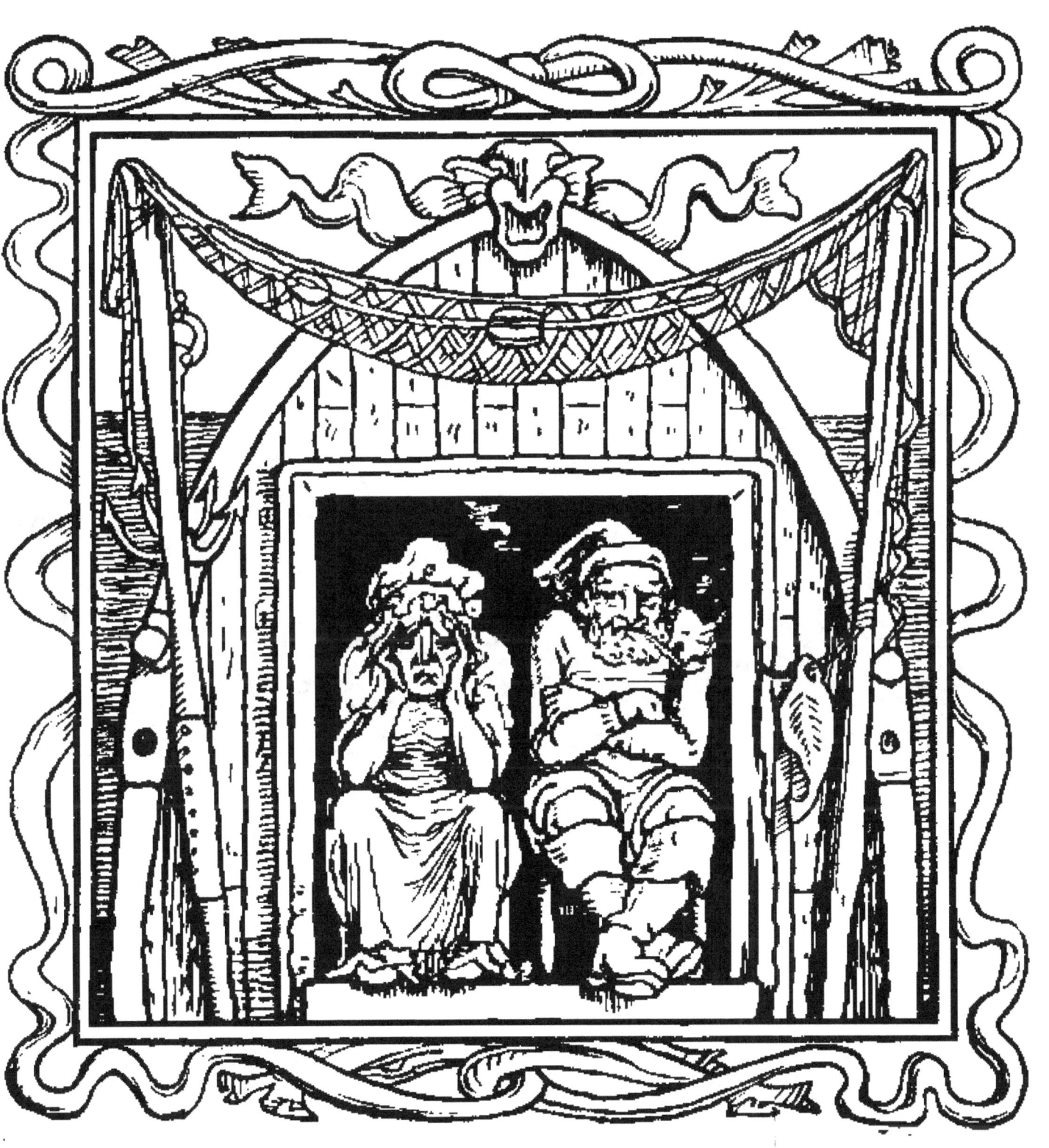

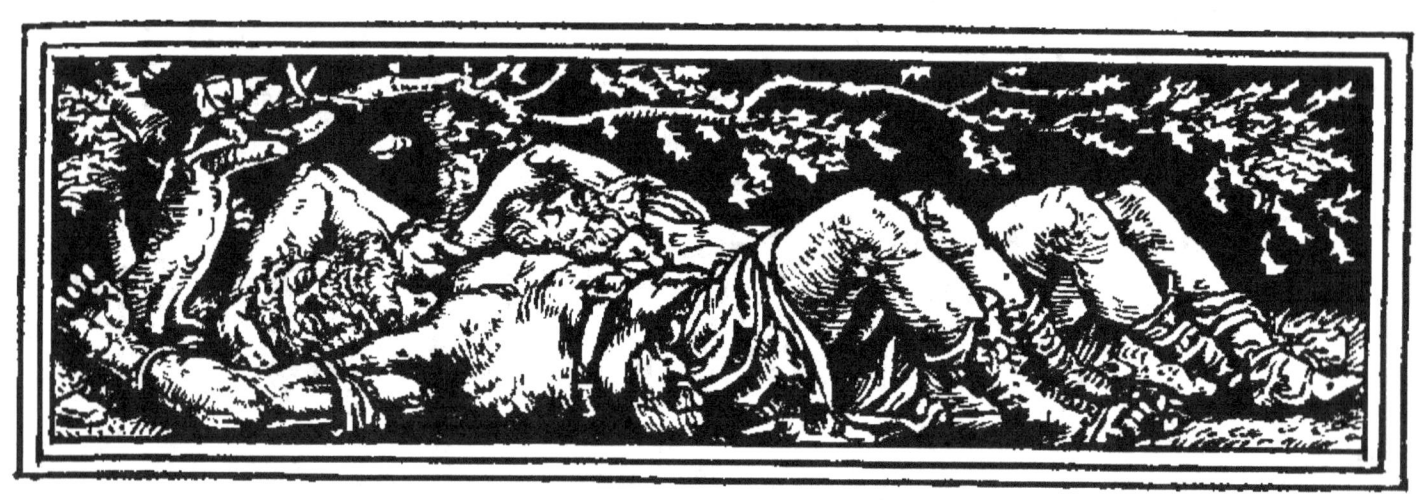

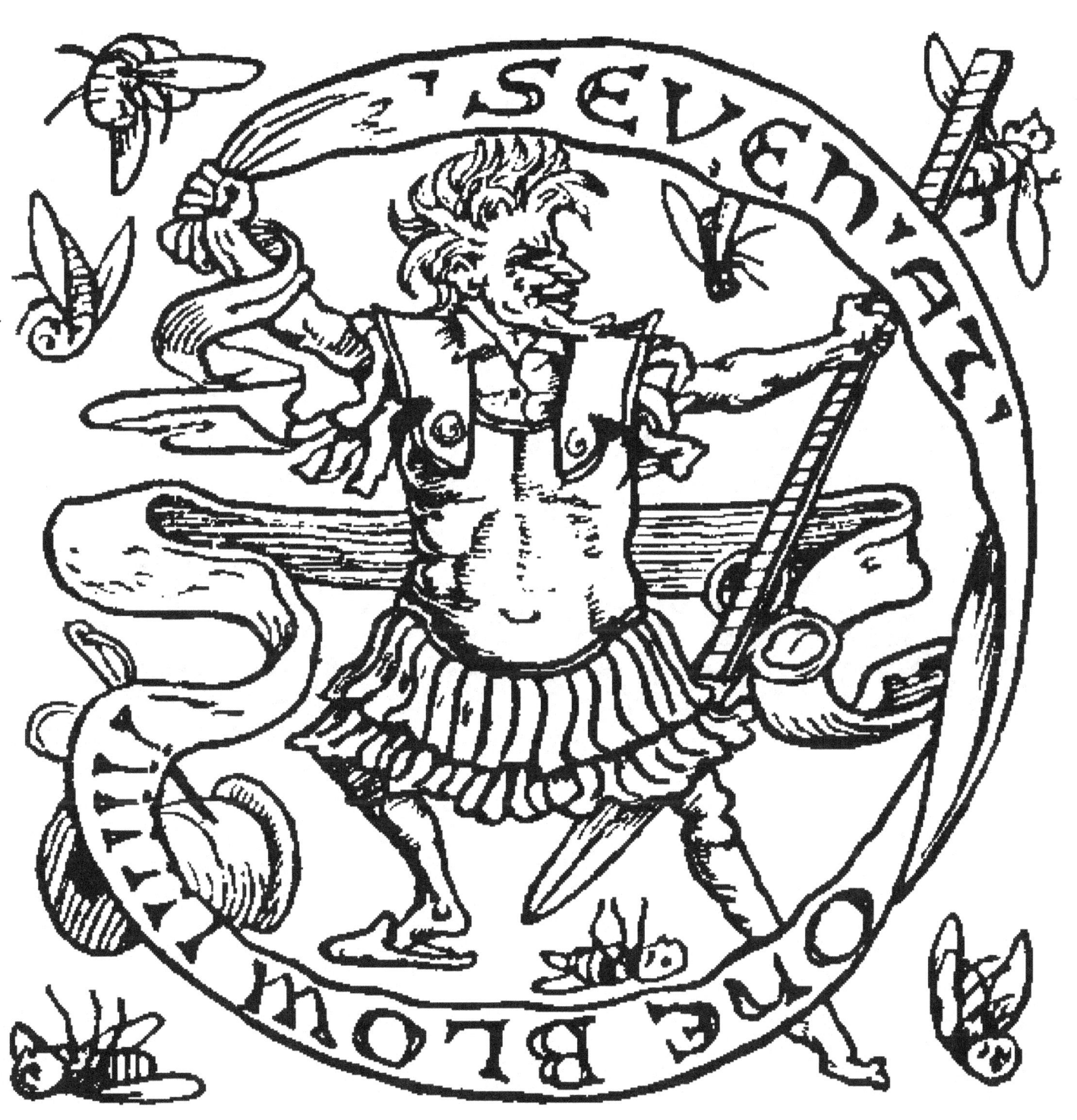

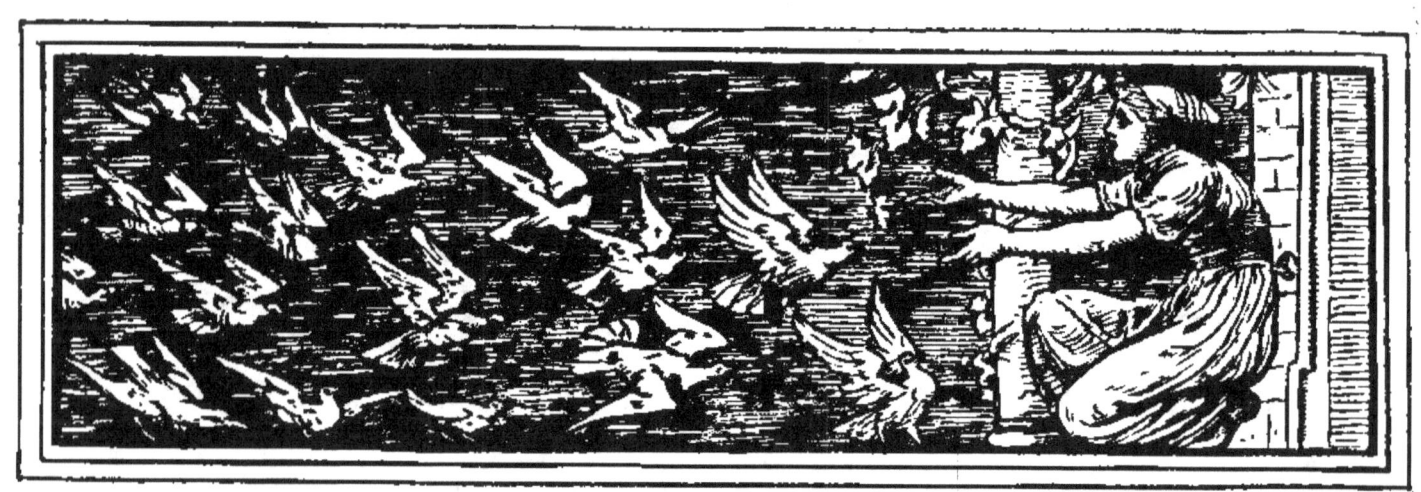

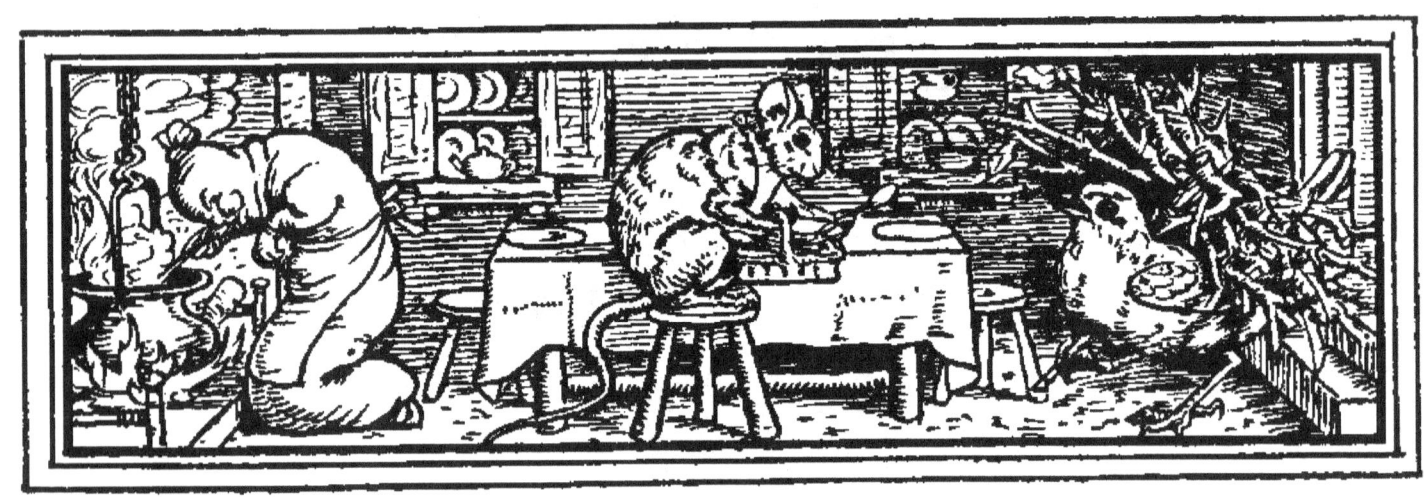

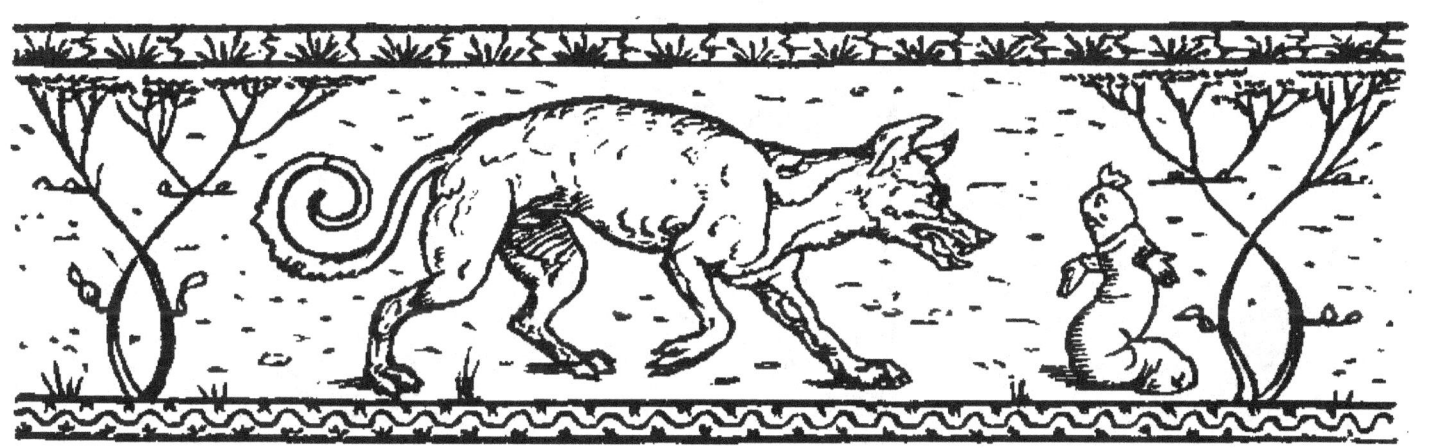

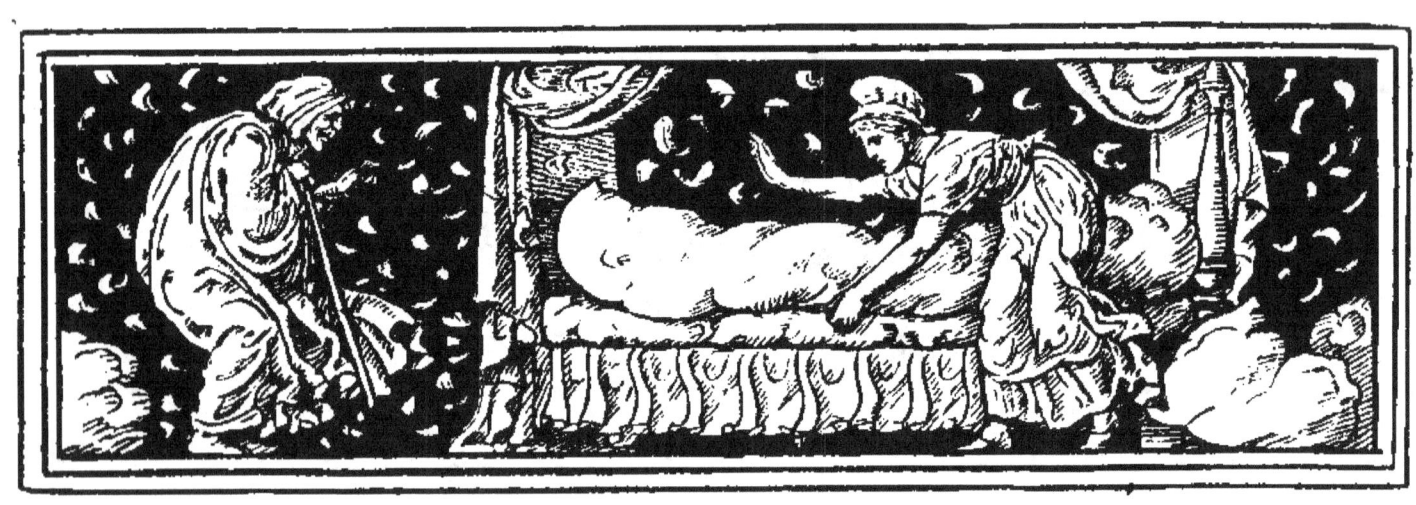

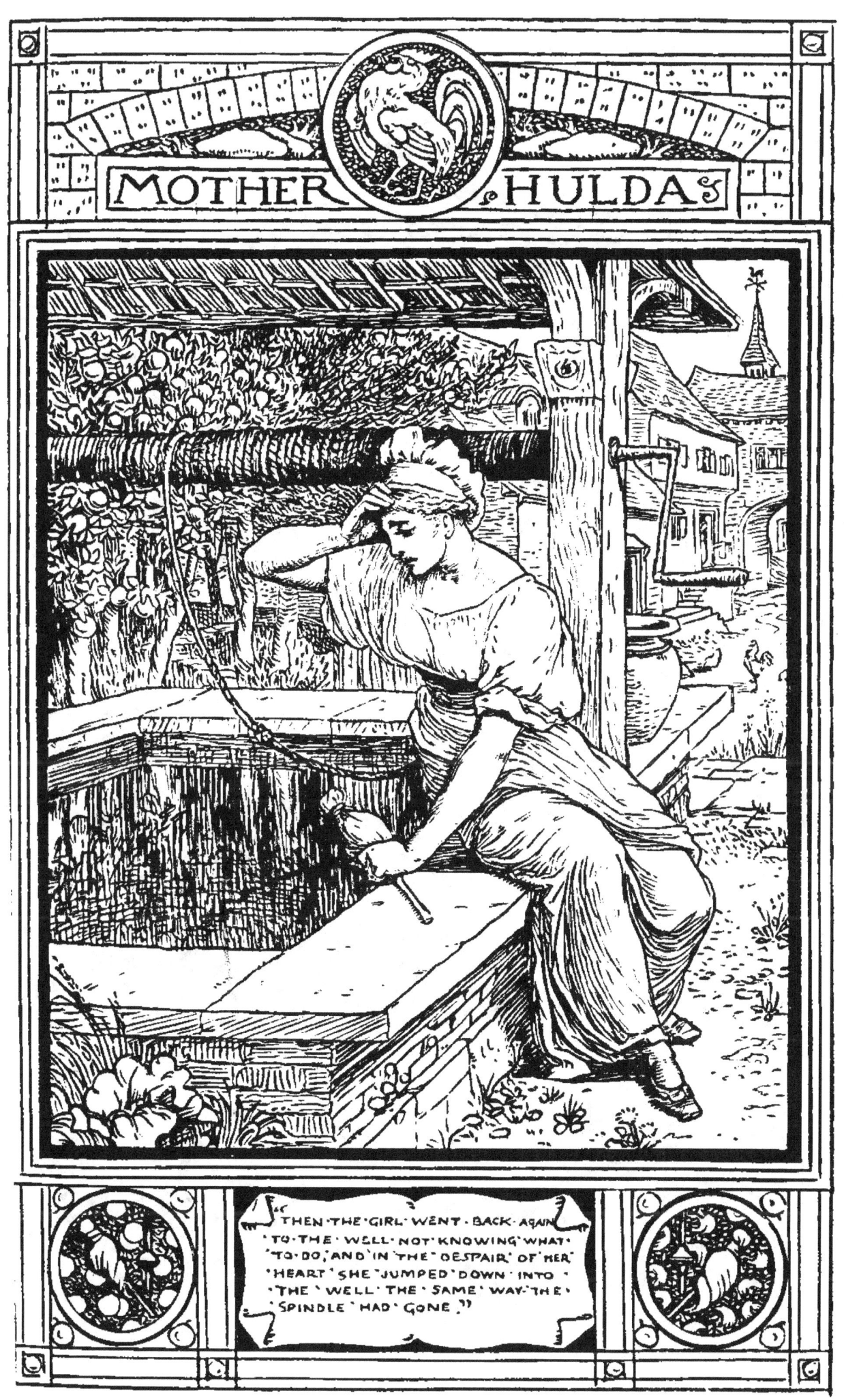

MOTHER HULDA

THEN·THE·GIRL·WENT·BACK·AGAIN
TO·THE·WELL·NOT·KNOWING·WHAT·
TO·DO, AND·IN·THE·DESPAIR·OF·HER·
HEART·SHE·JUMPED·DOWN·INTO·
THE·WELL·THE·SAME·WAY·THE·
SPINDLE·HAD·GONE."

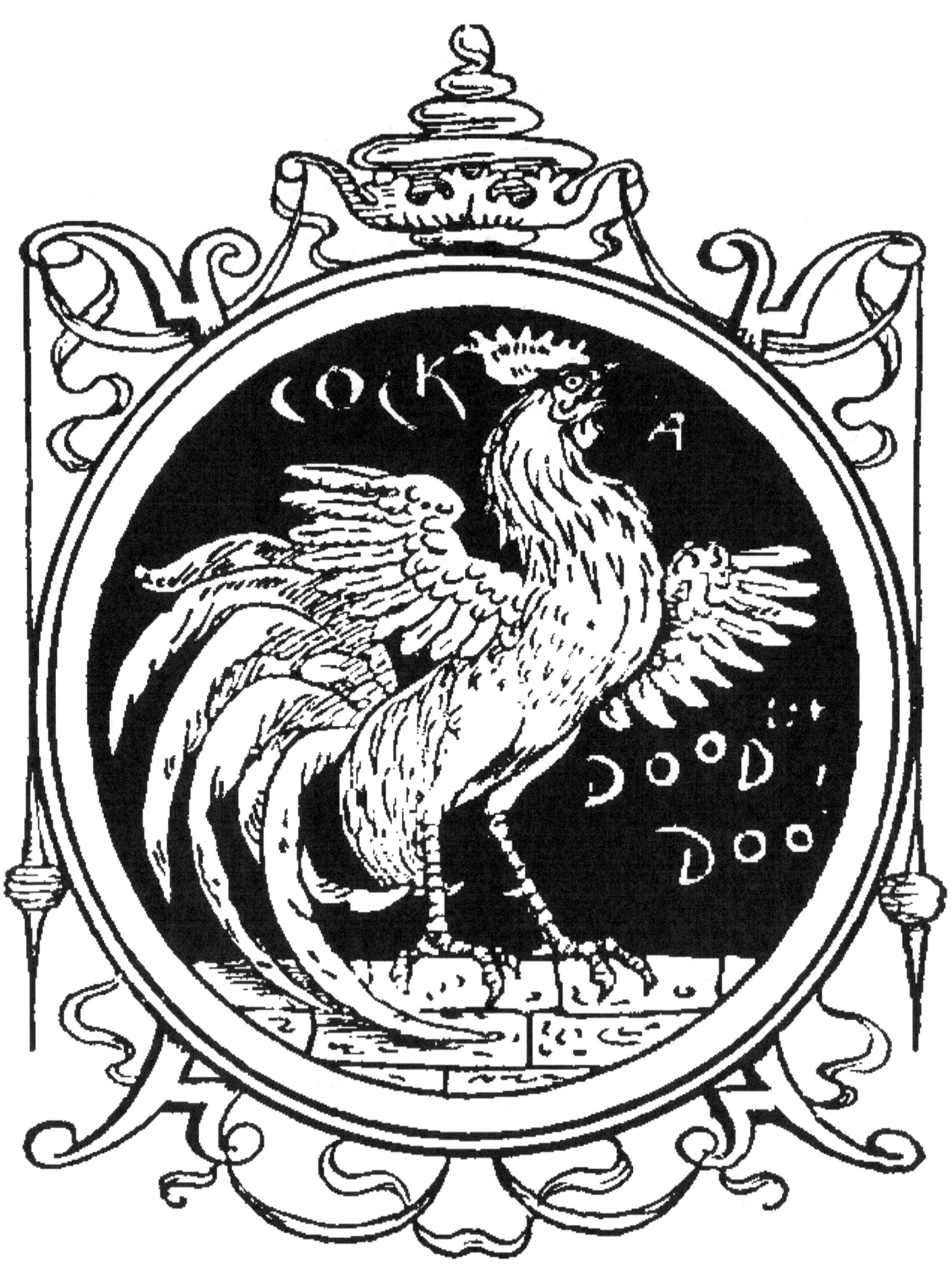

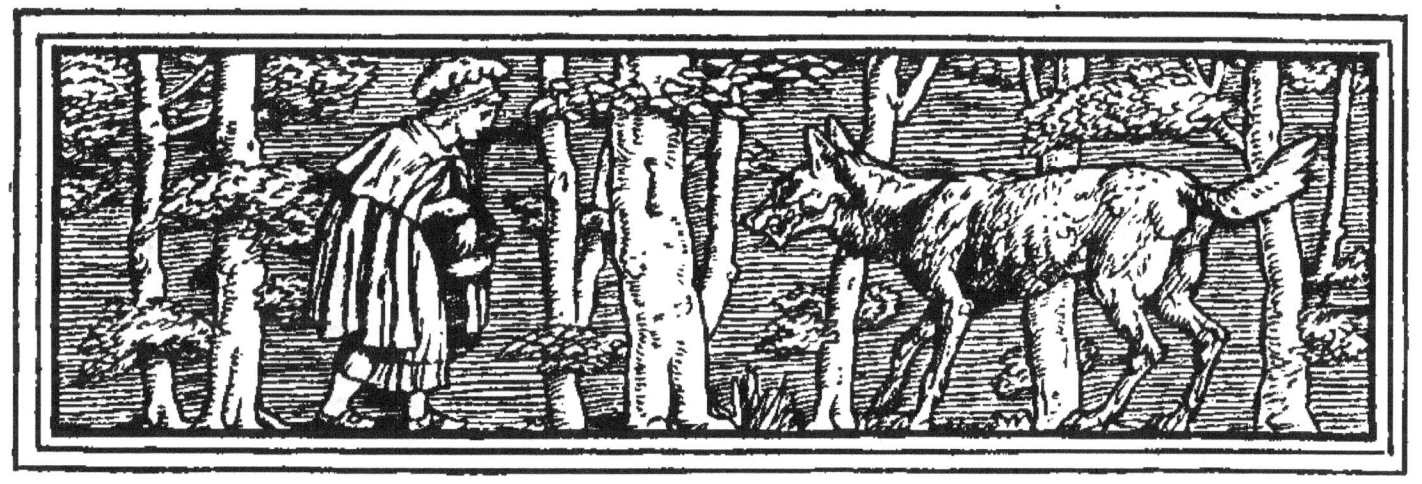

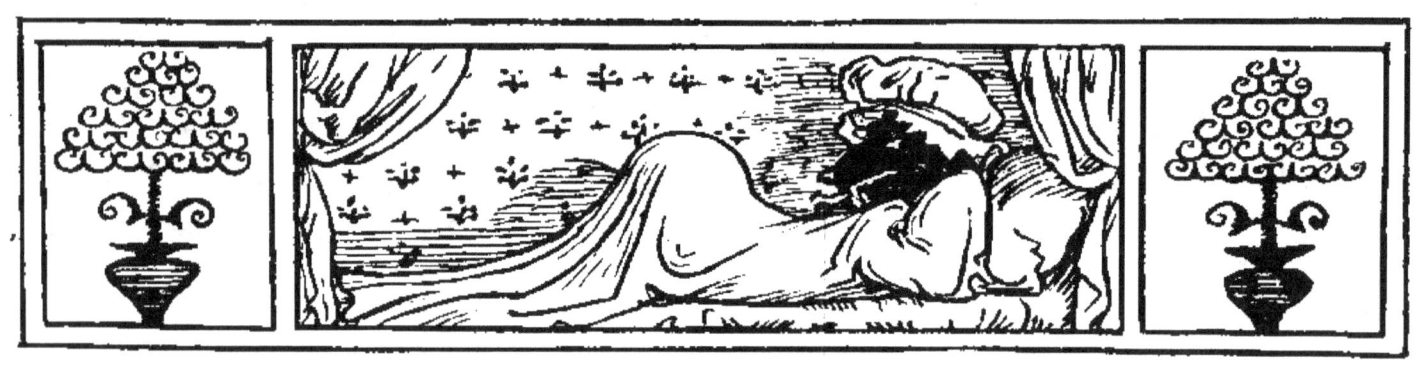

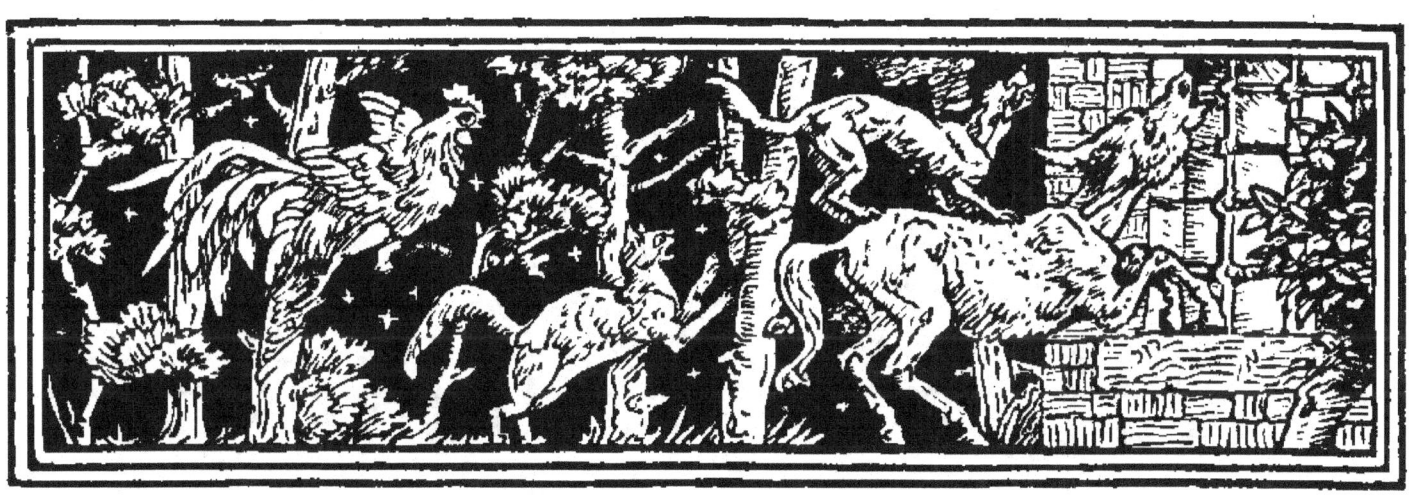

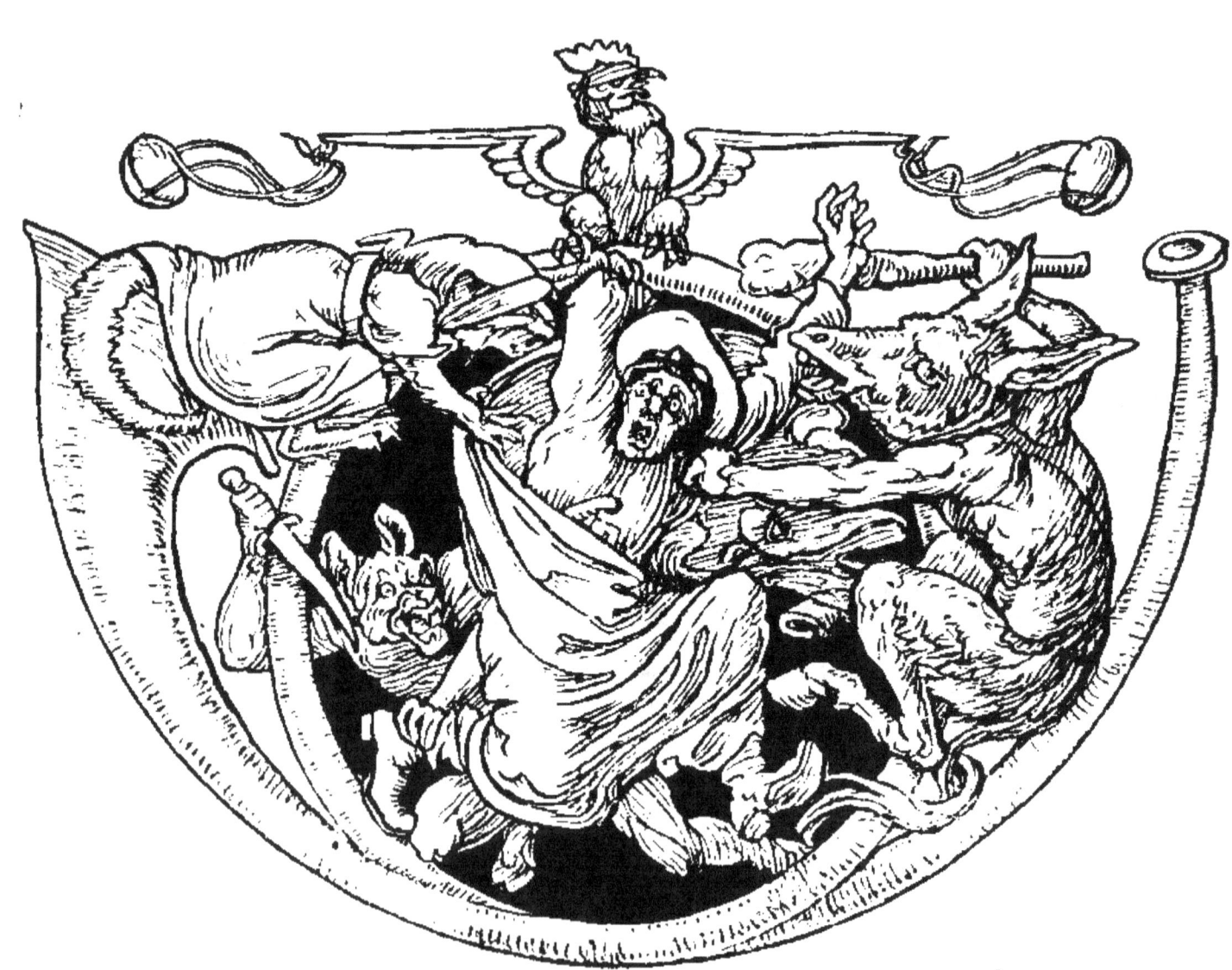

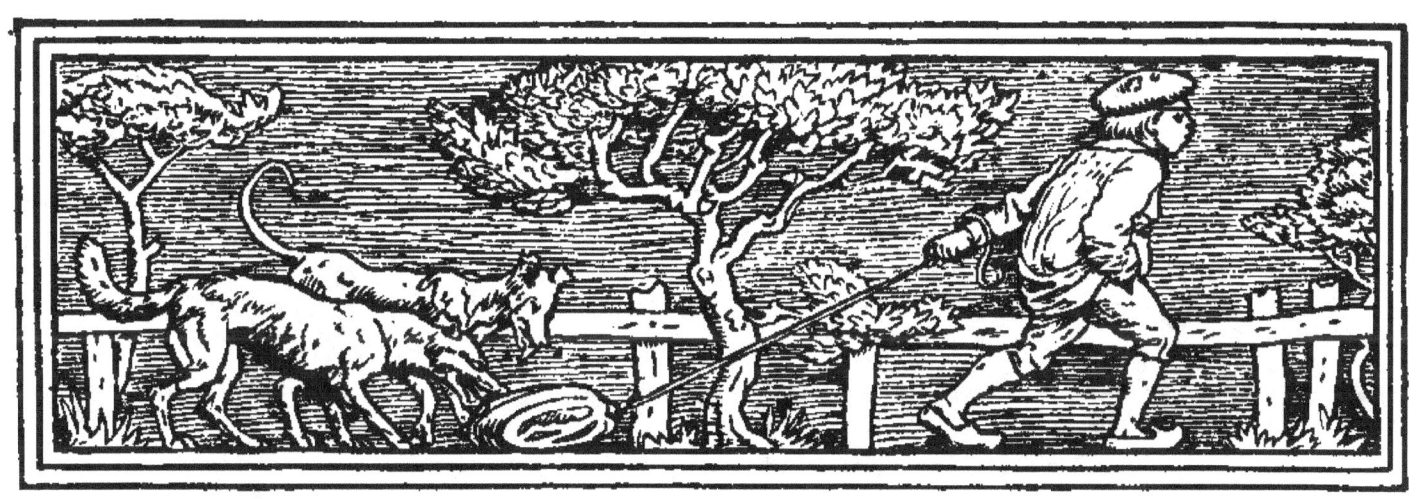

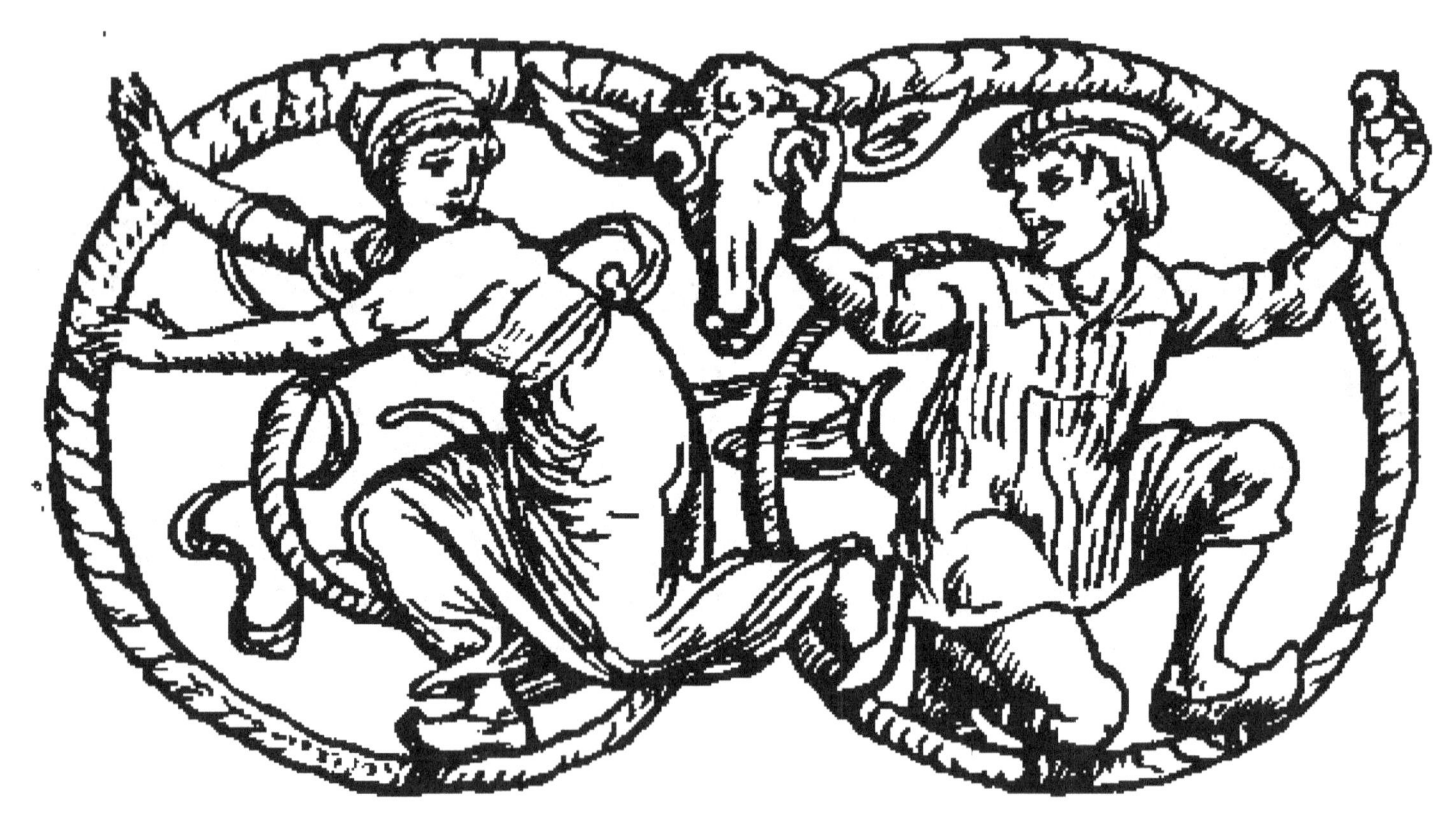

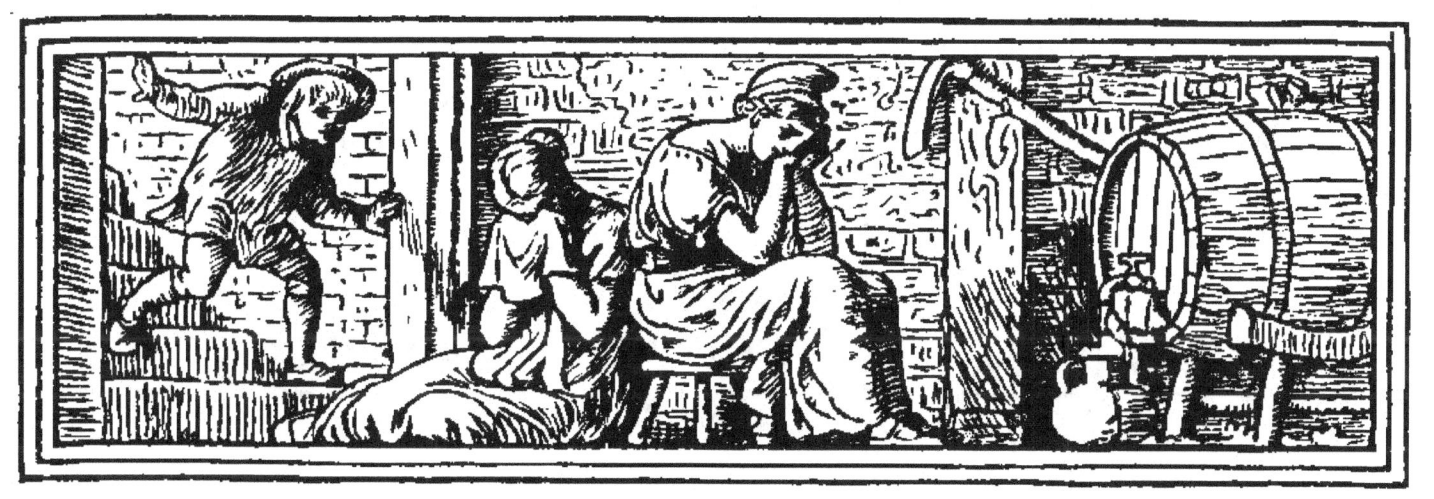

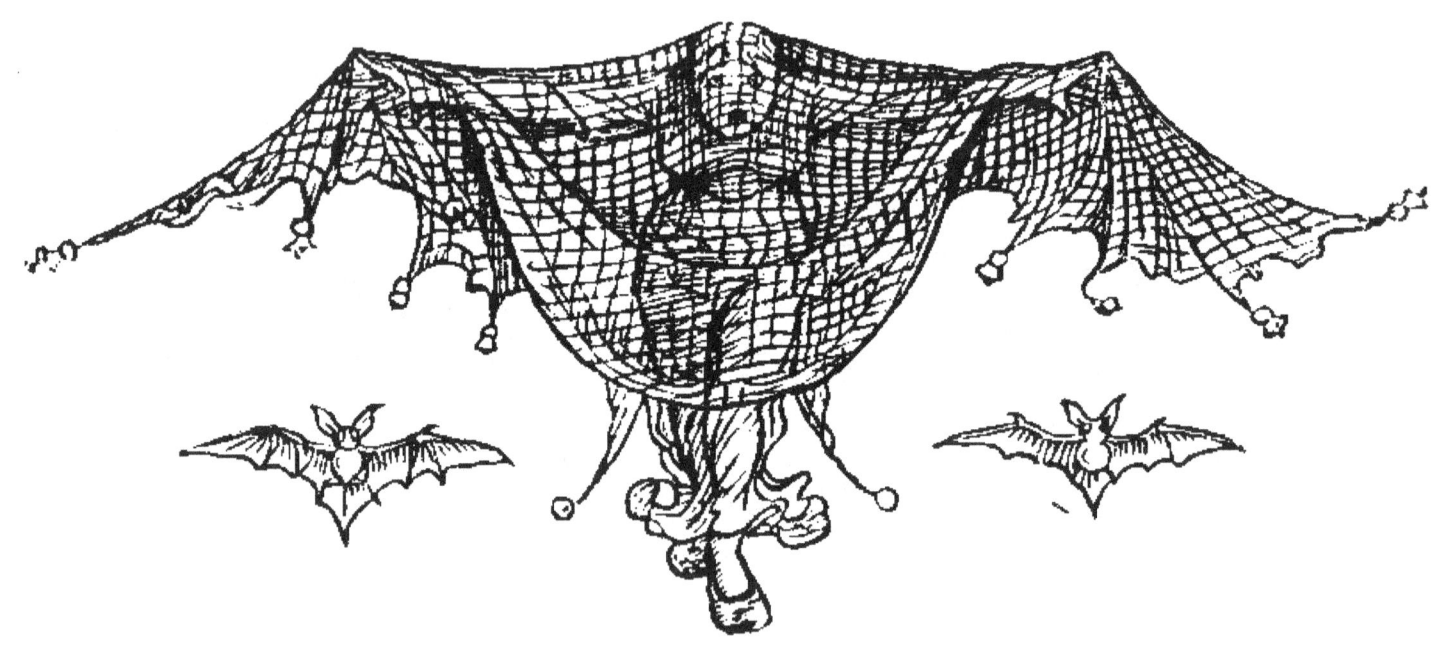

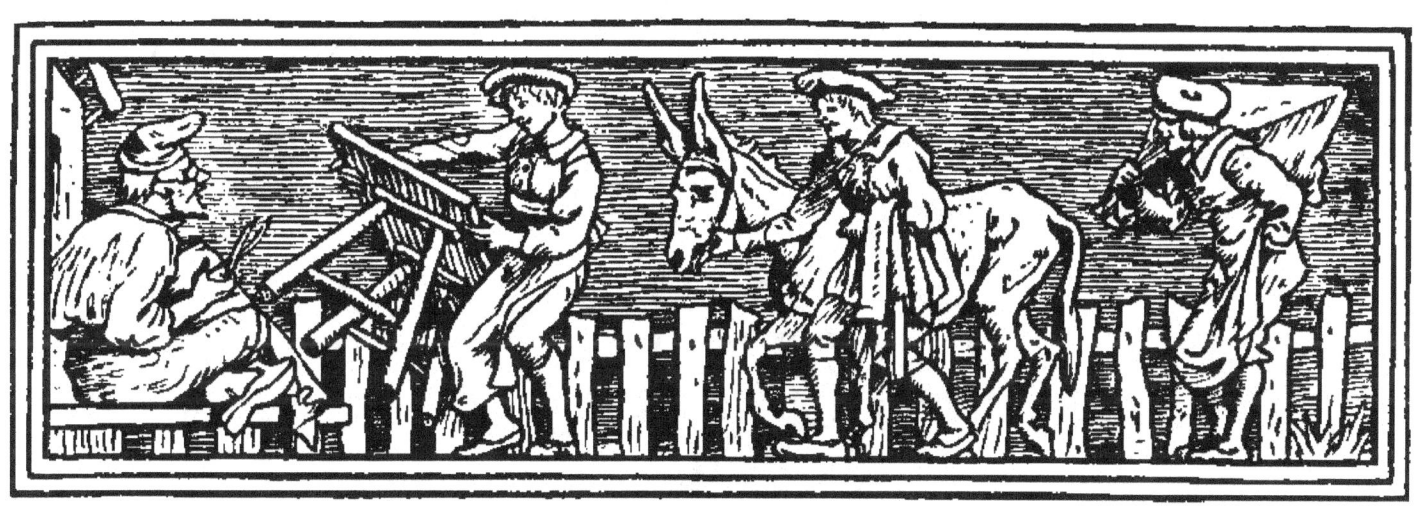

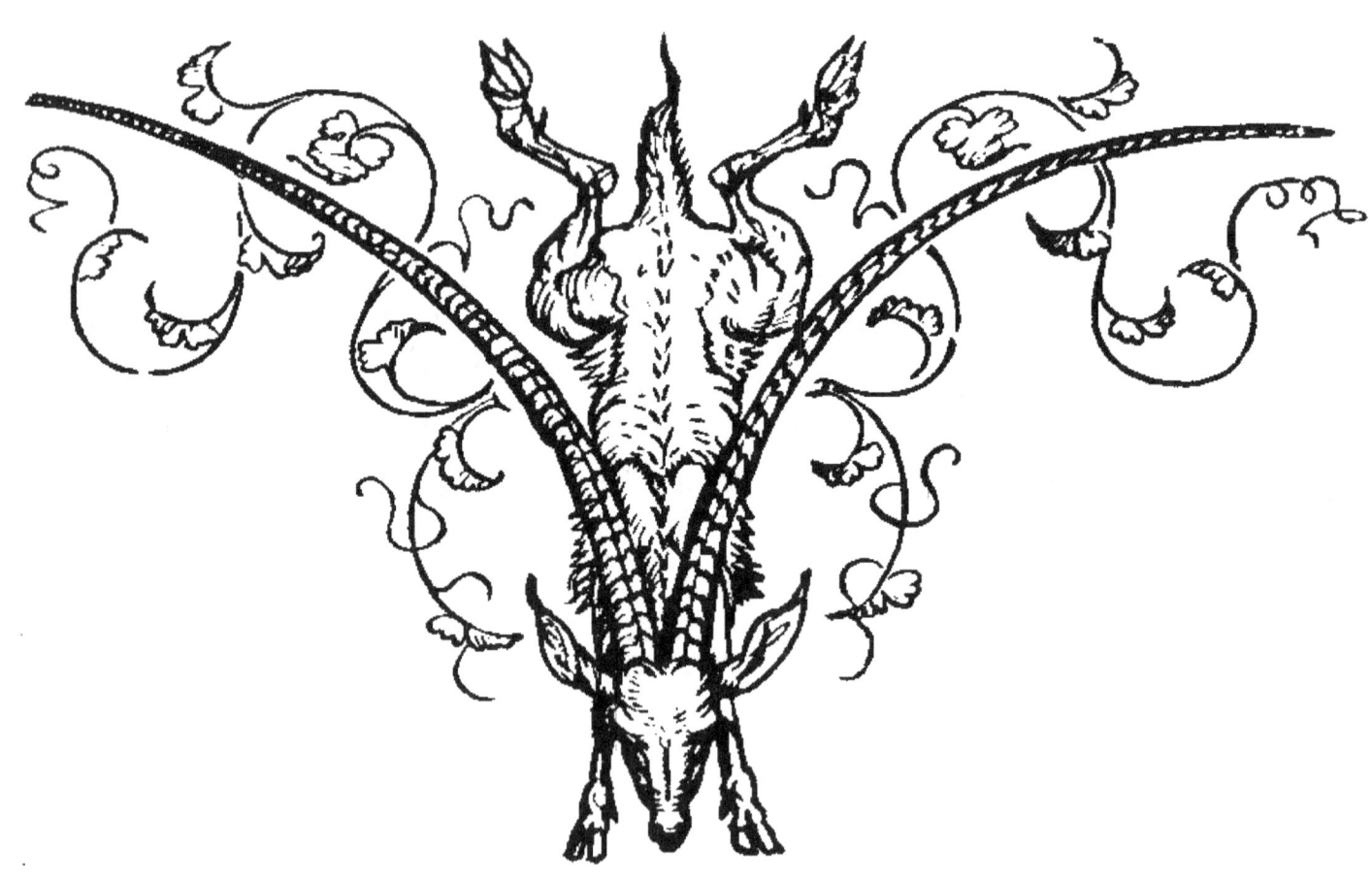

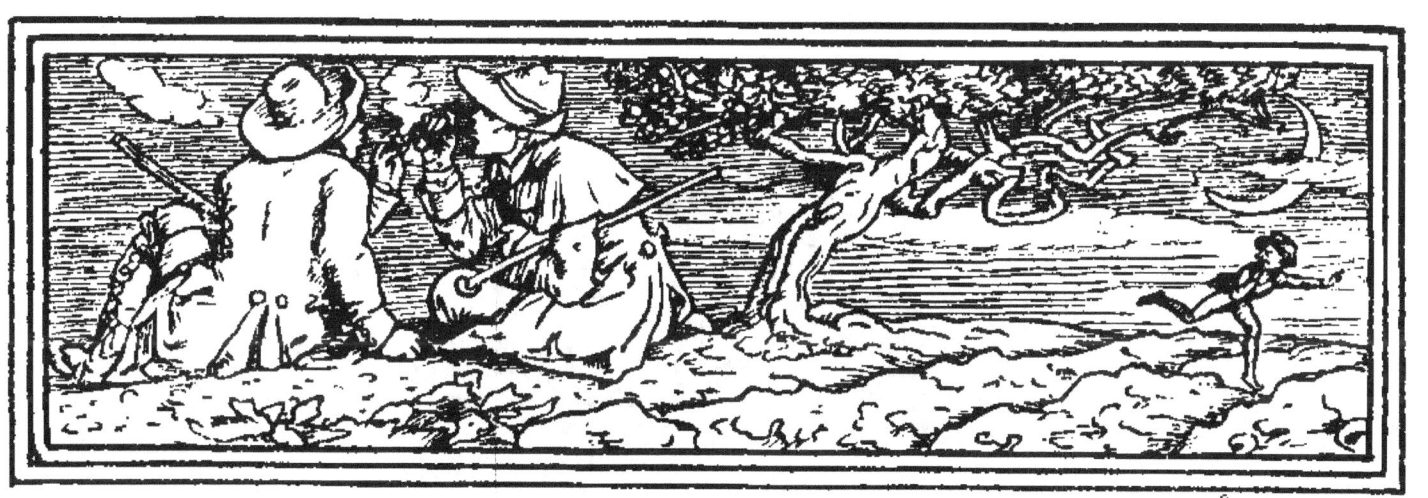

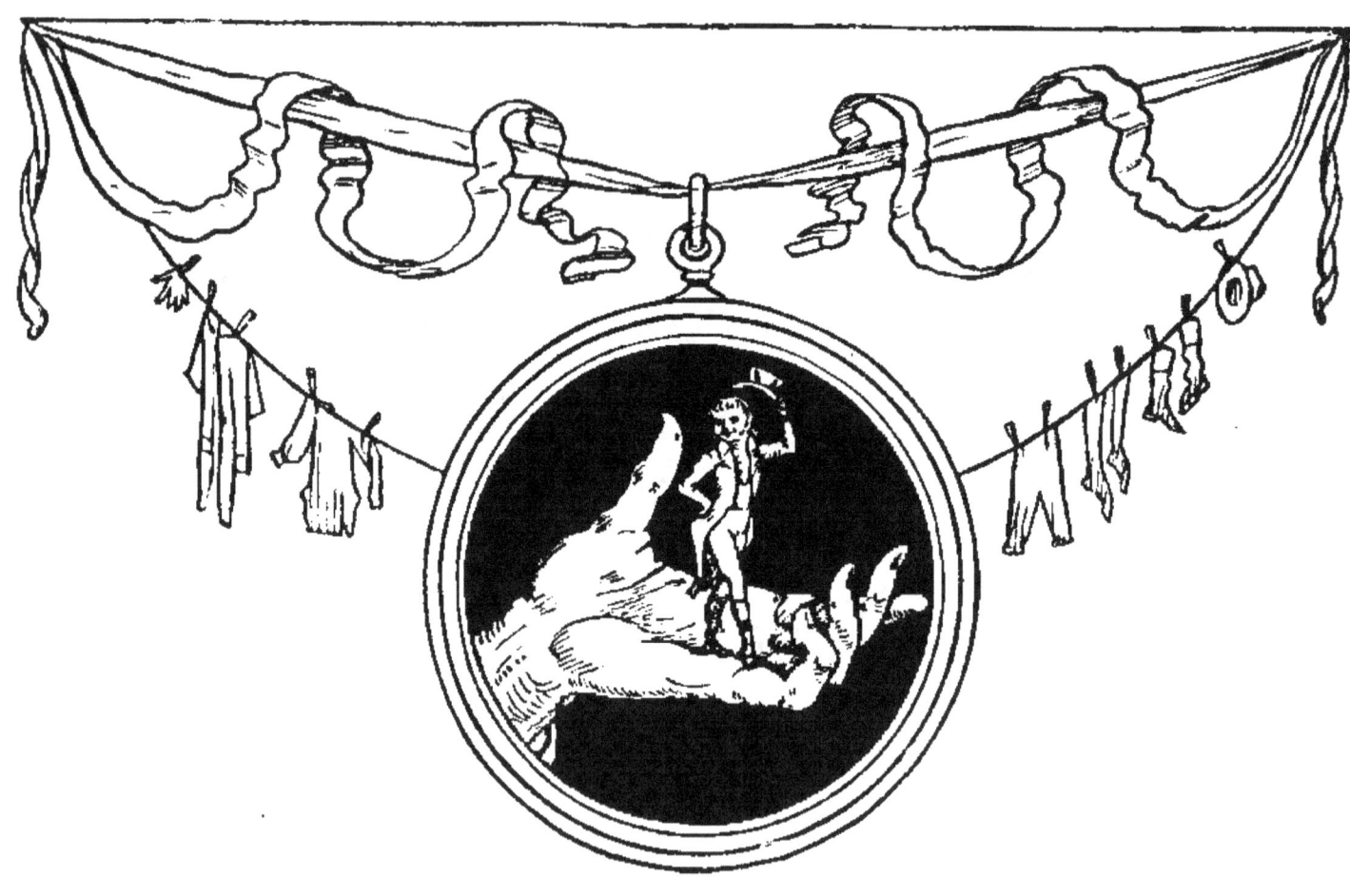

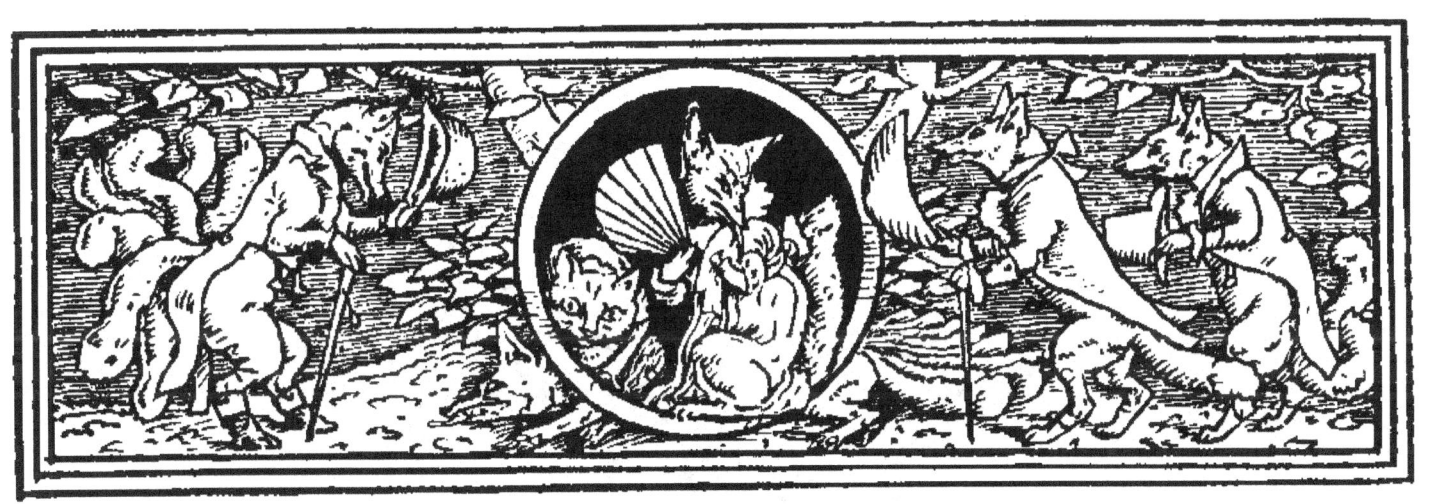

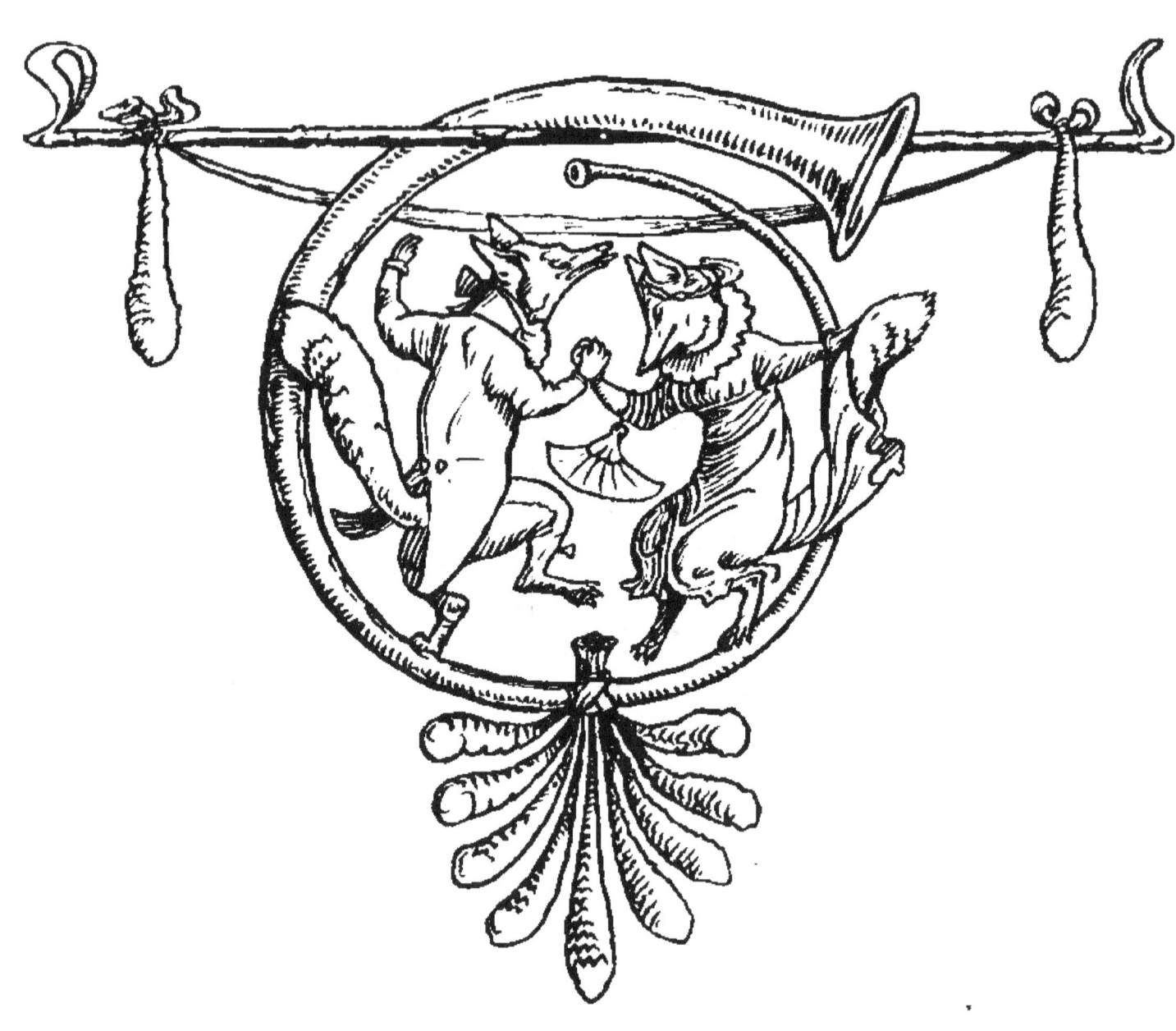

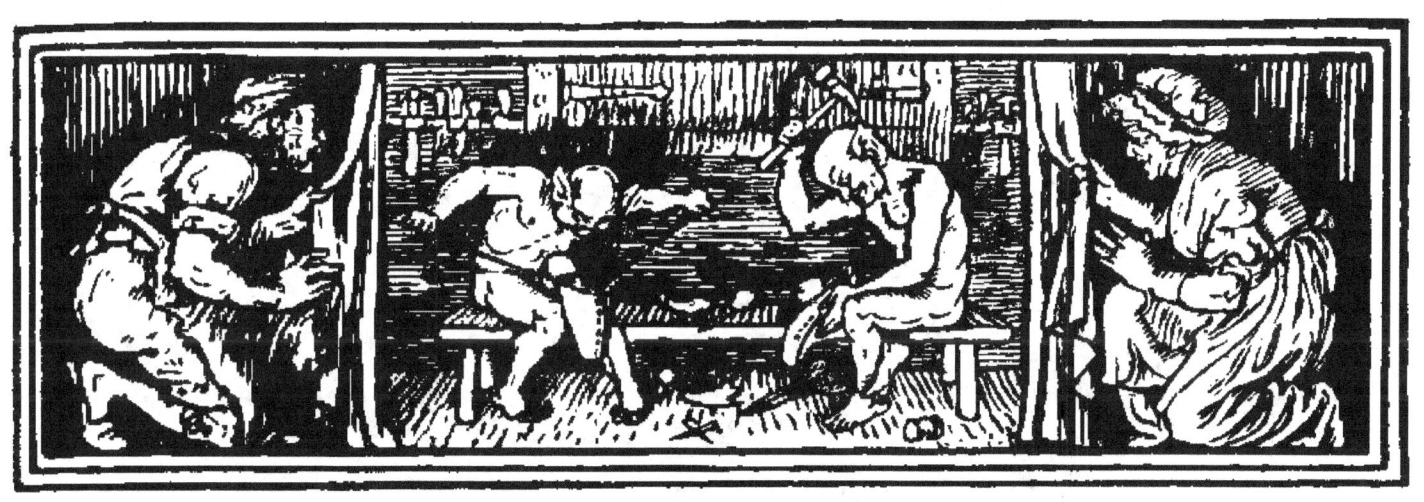

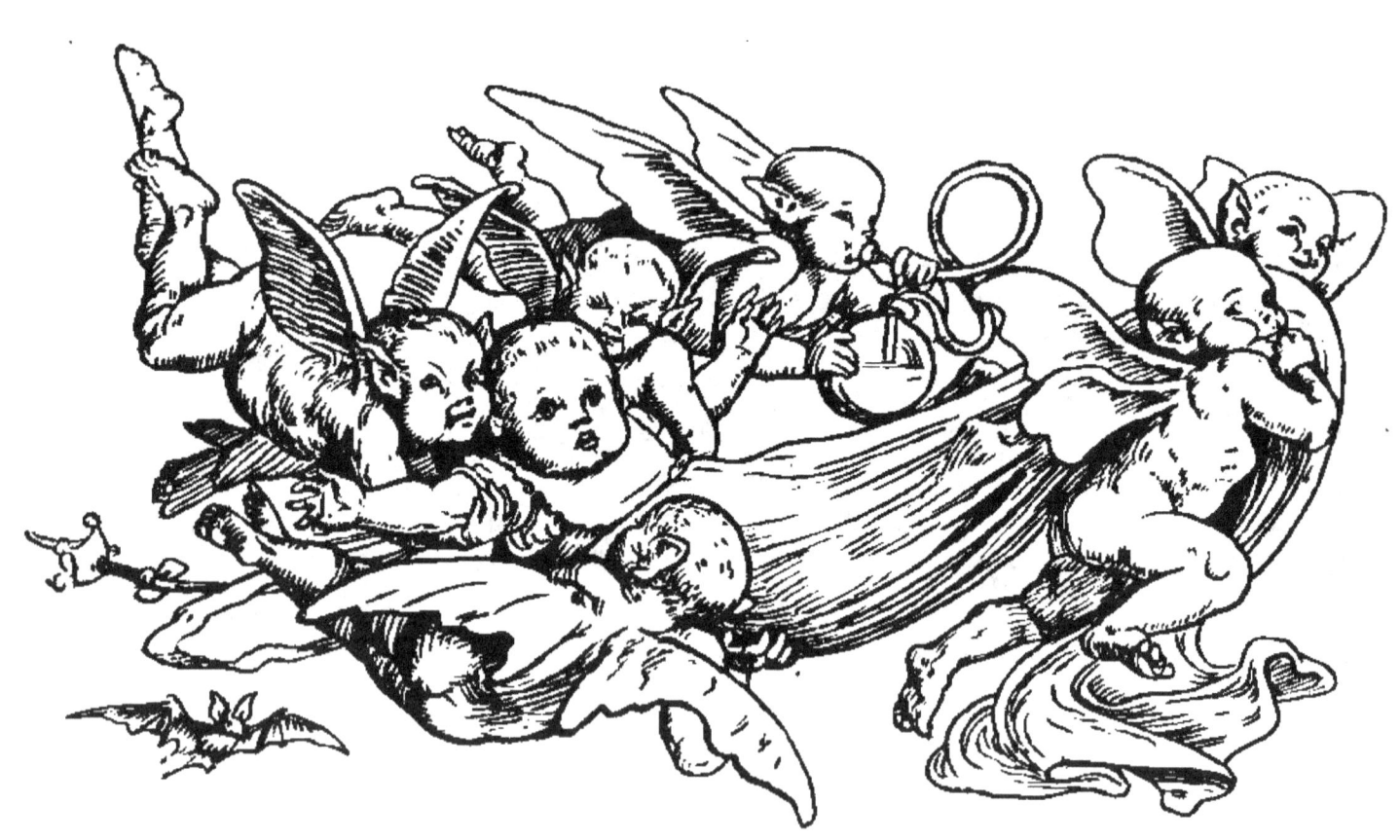

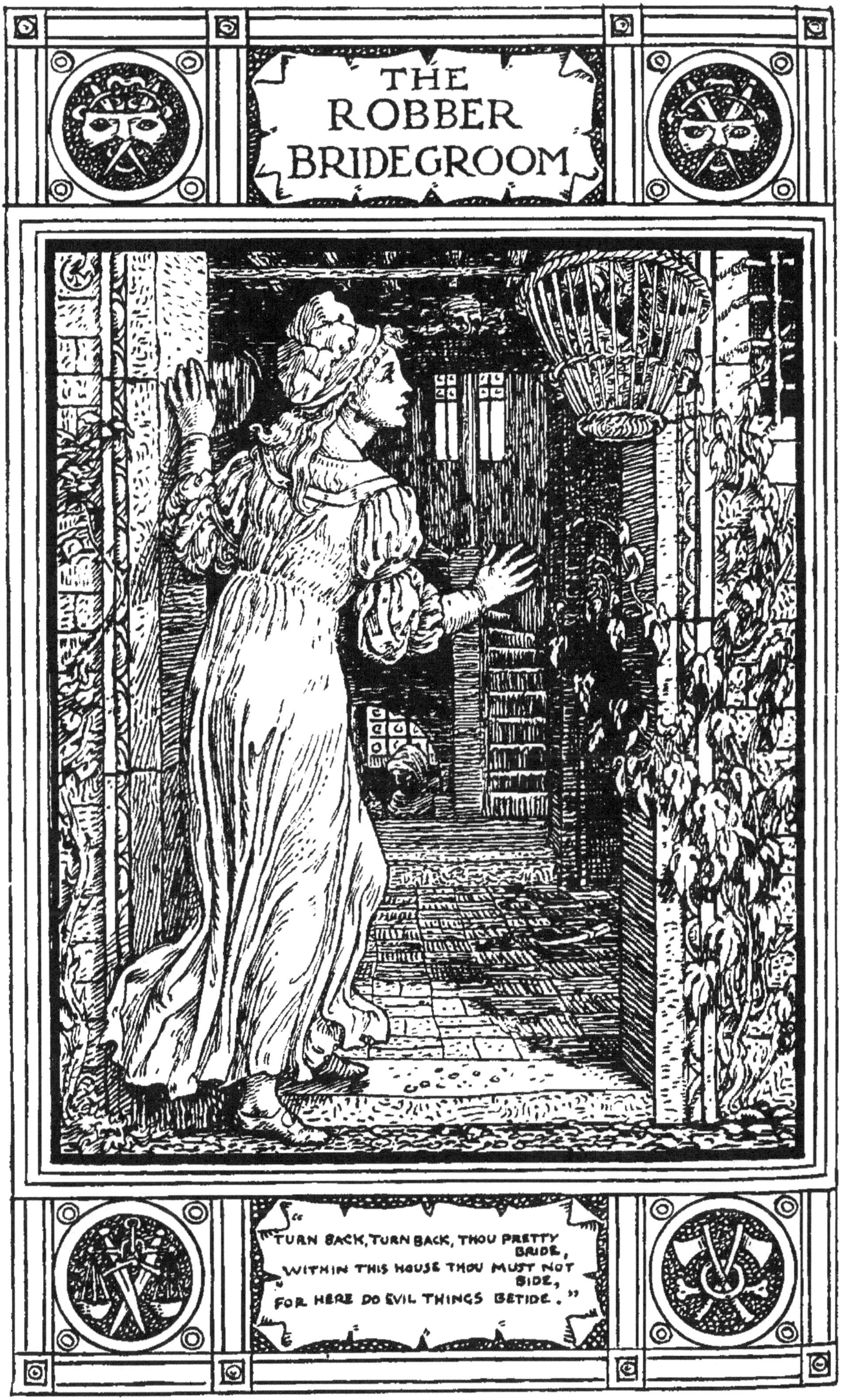

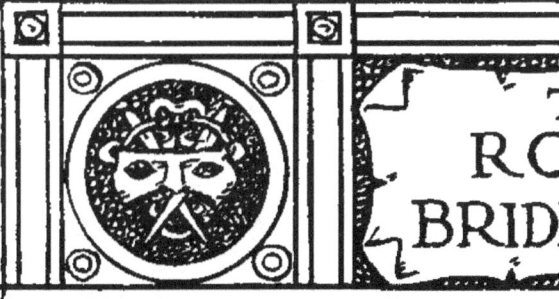

THE ROBBER BRIDEGROOM

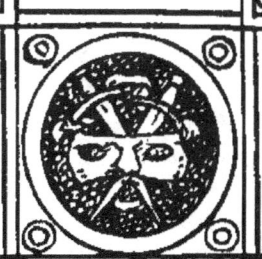

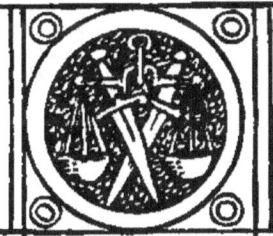

"TURN BACK, TURN BACK, THOU PRETTY BRIDE,
WITHIN THIS HOUSE THOU MUST NOT BIDE,
FOR HERE DO EVIL THINGS BETIDE."

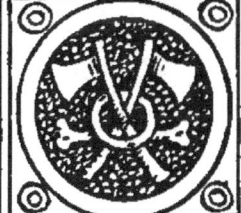

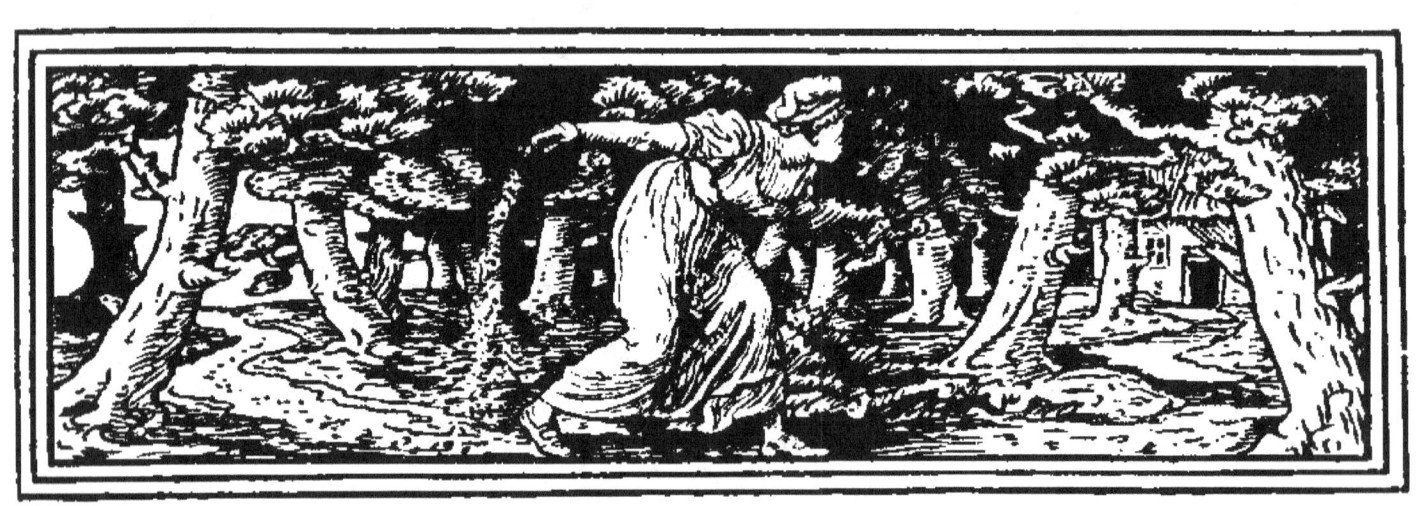

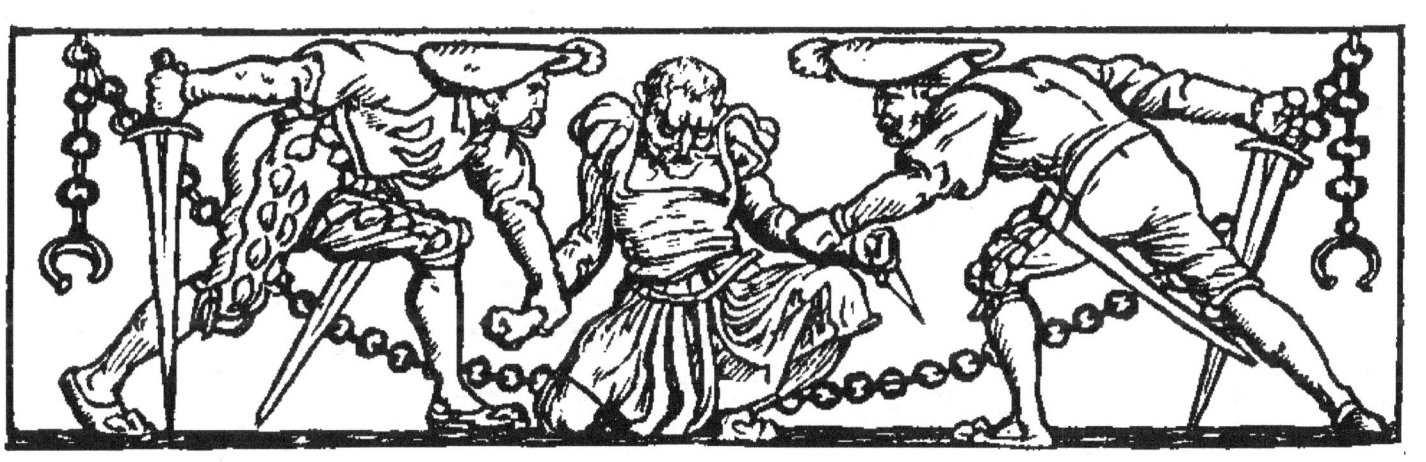

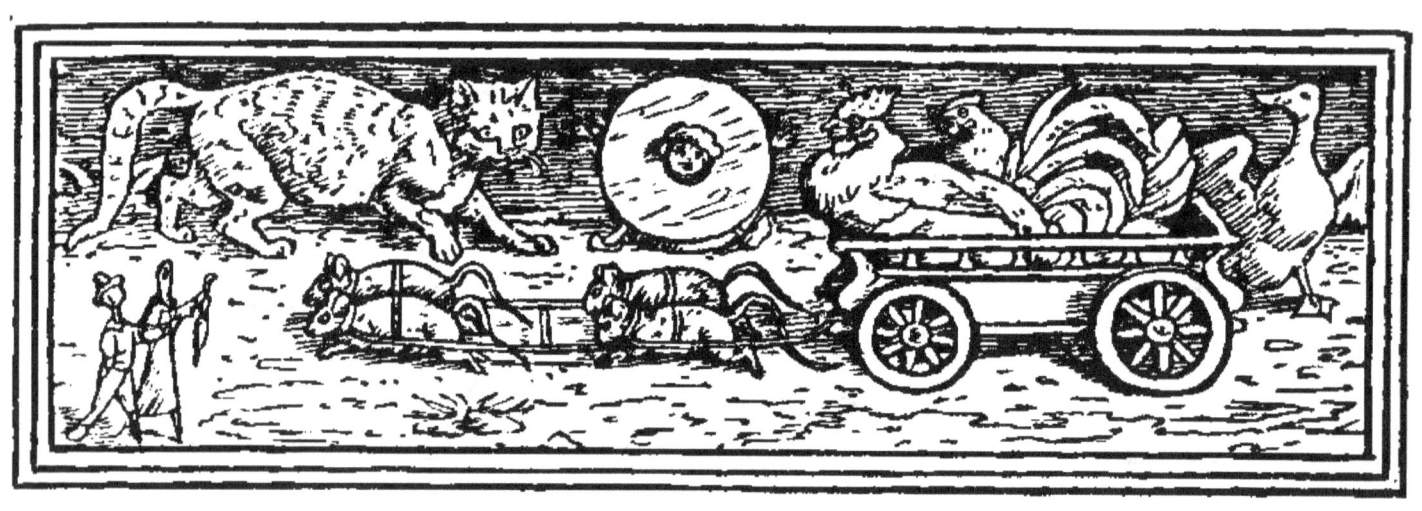

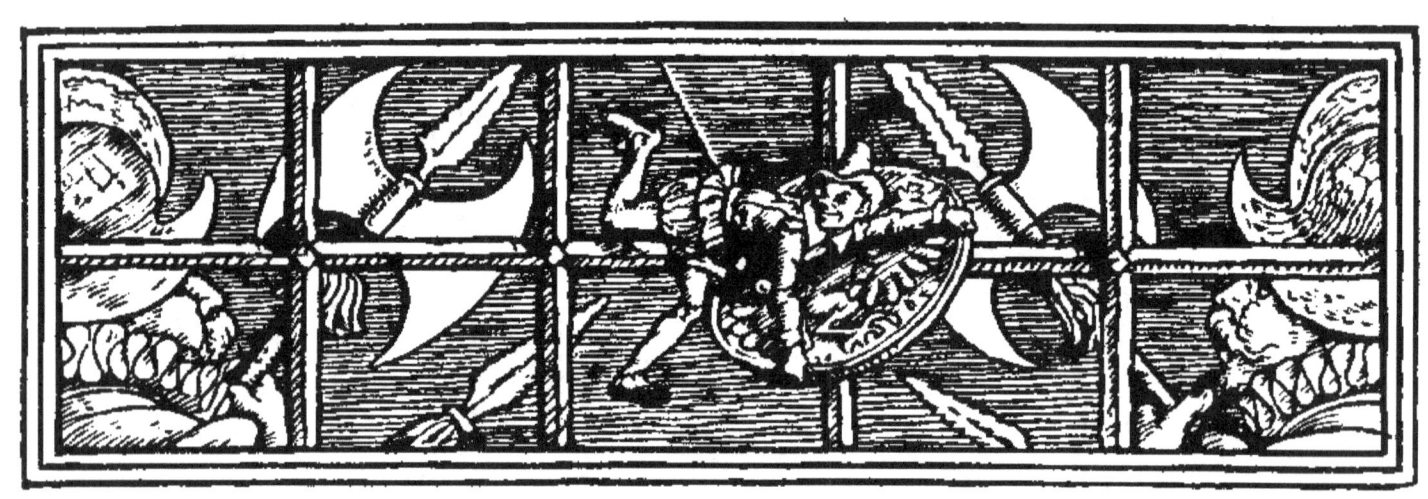

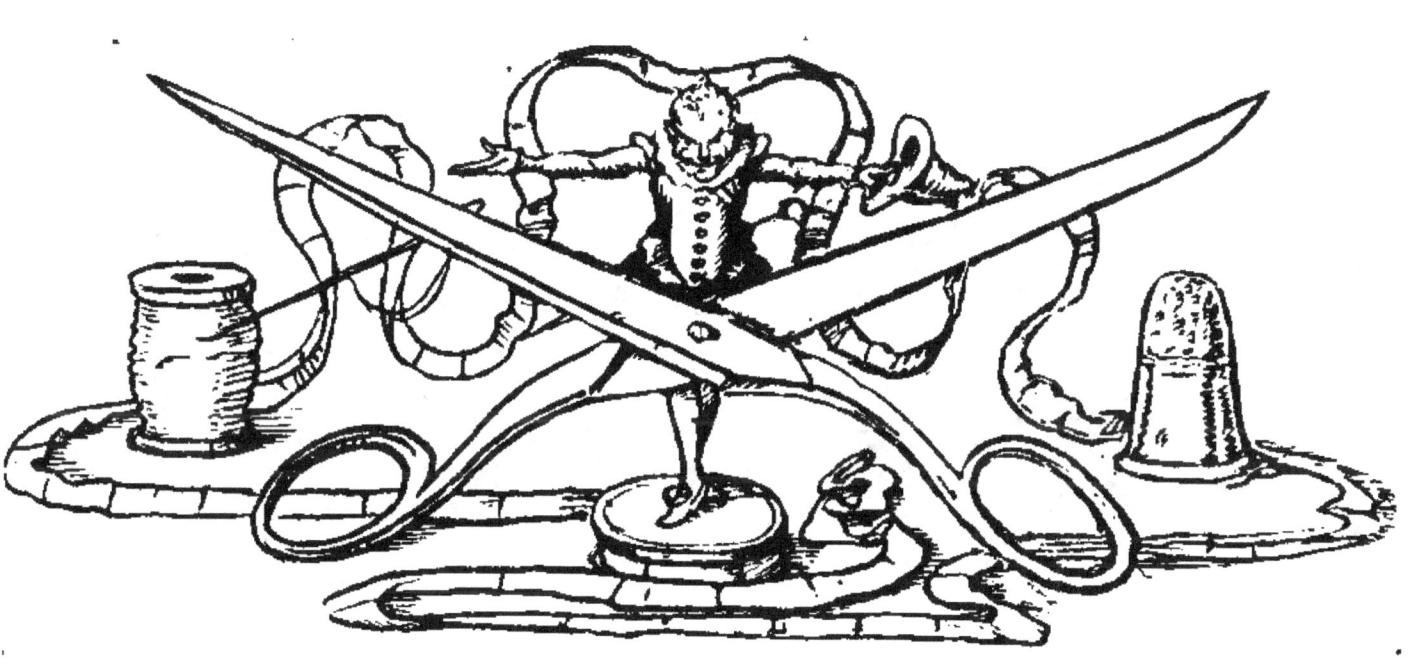

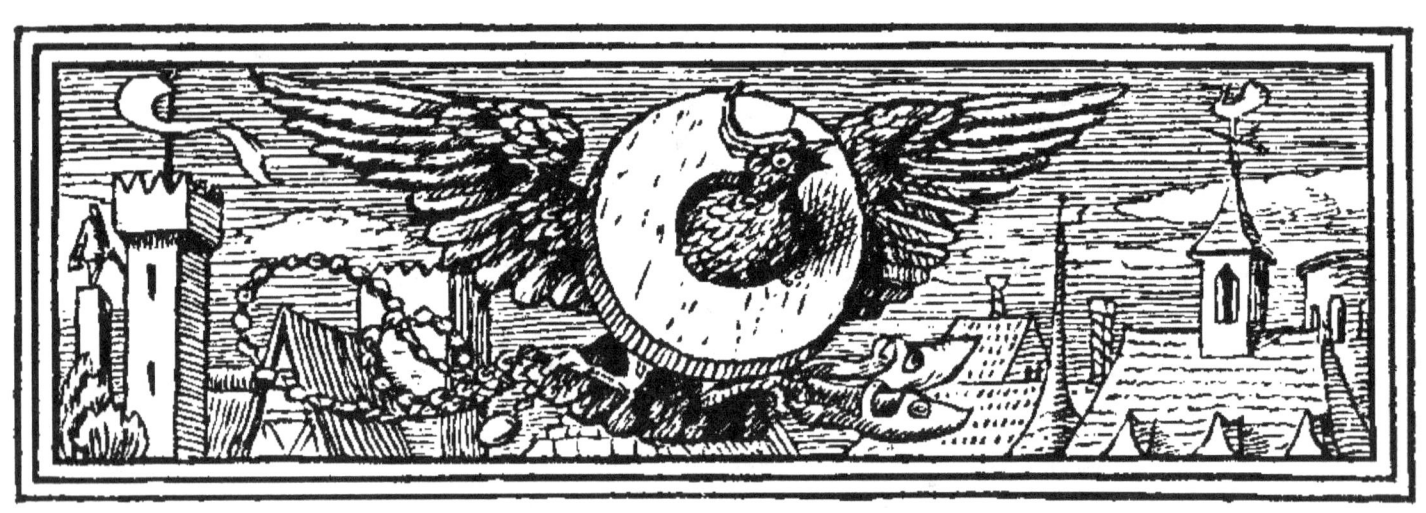

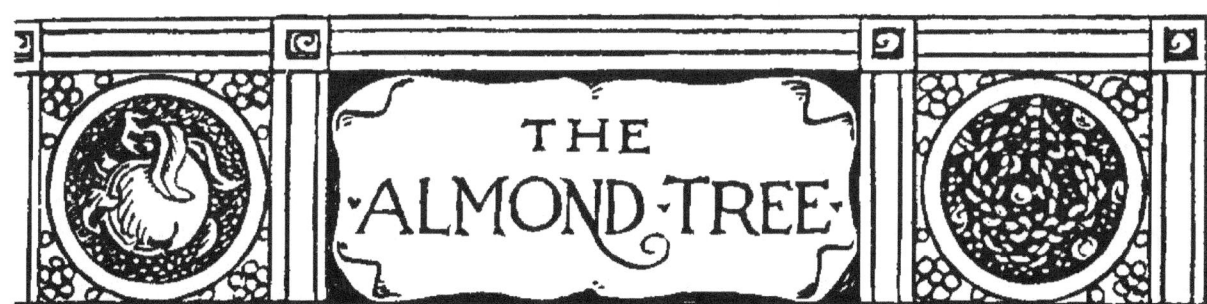

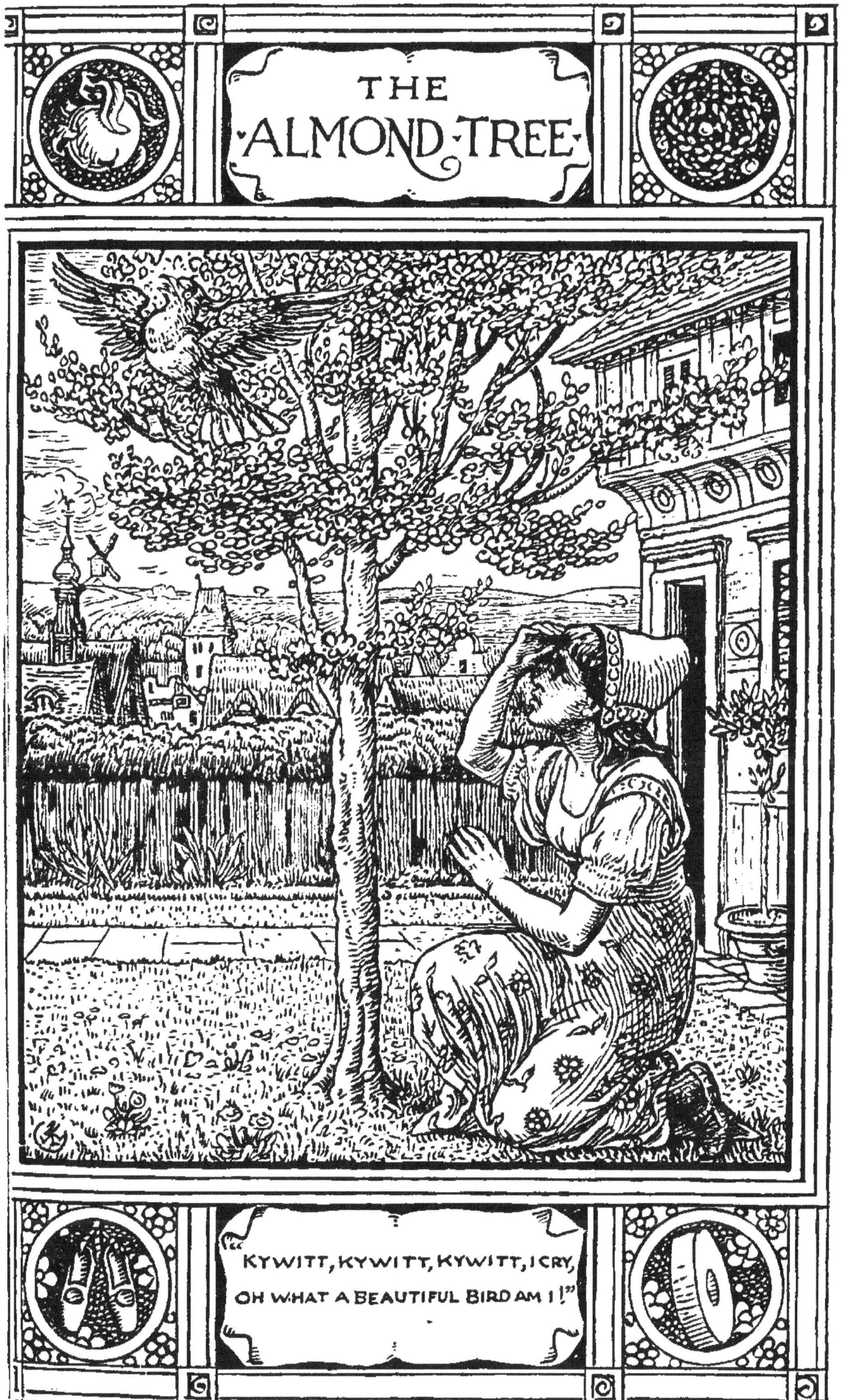

THE ALMOND·TREE

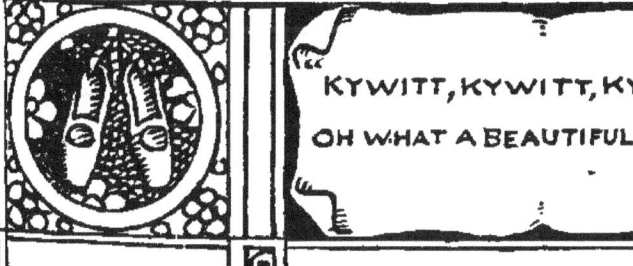

"KYWITT, KYWITT, KYWITT, I CRY,
OH WHAT A BEAUTIFUL BIRD AM I!"

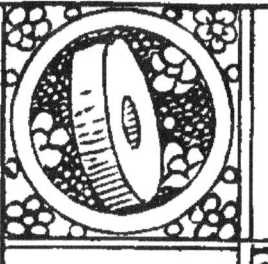

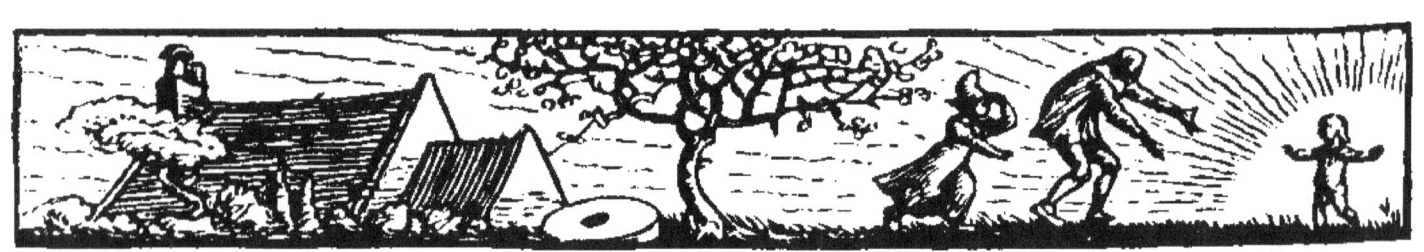

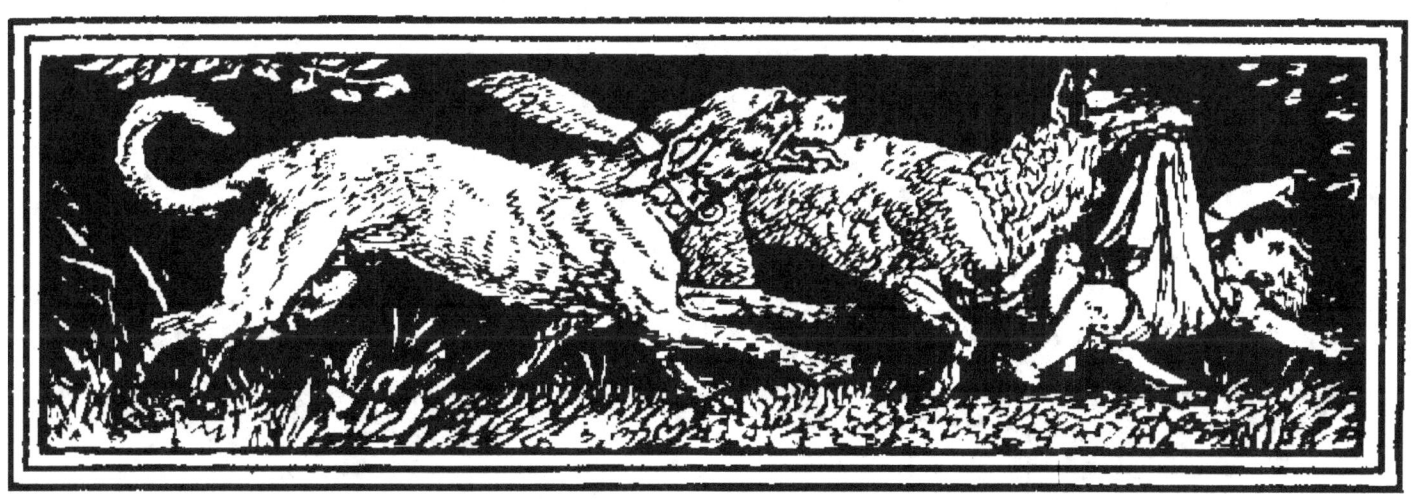

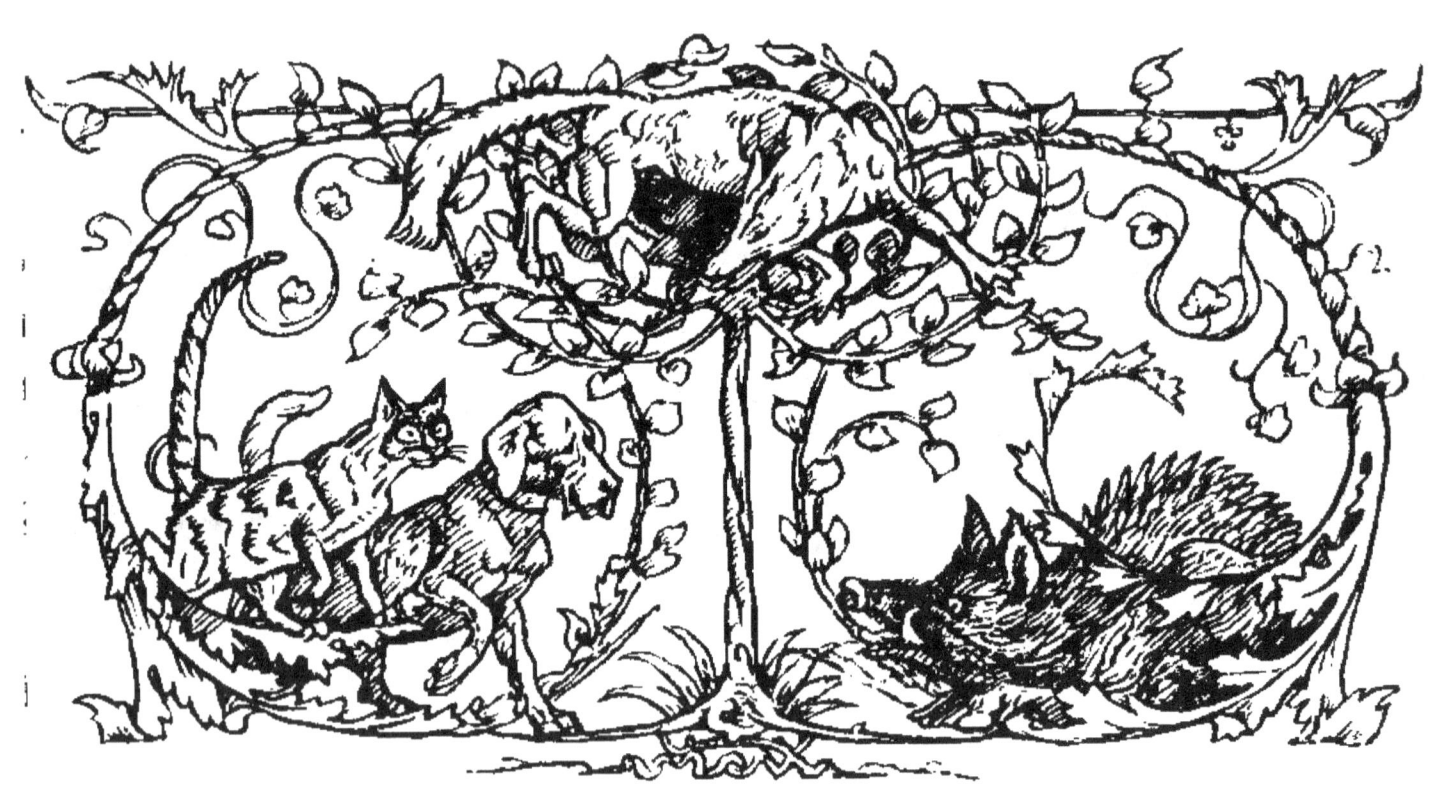

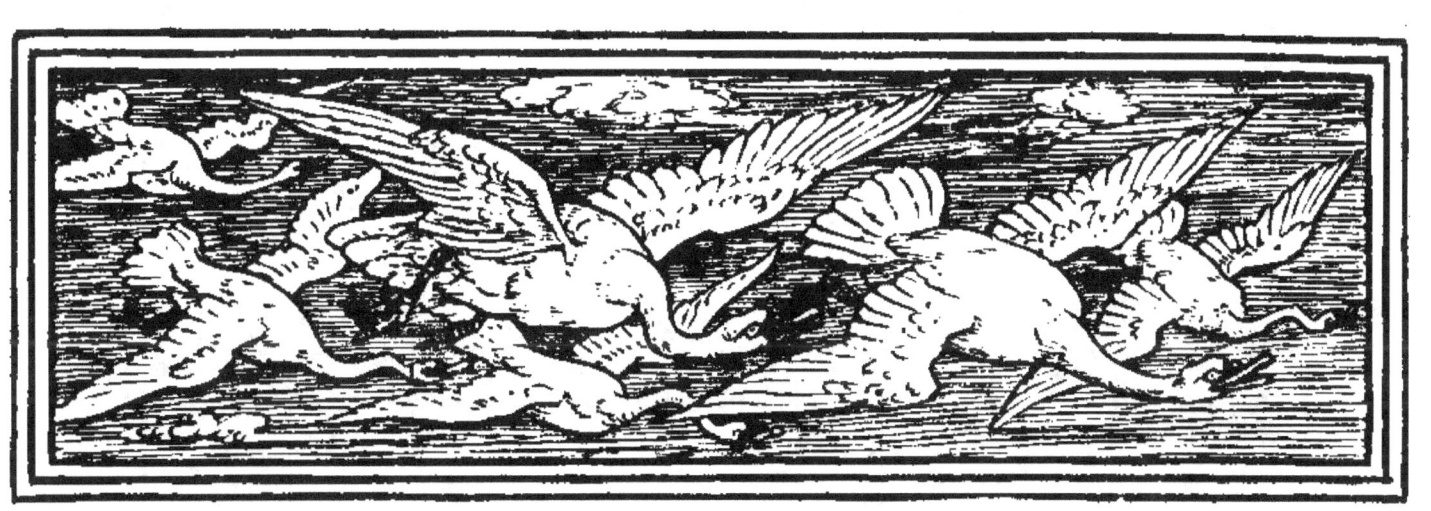

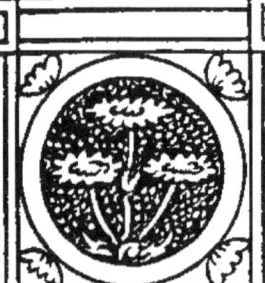
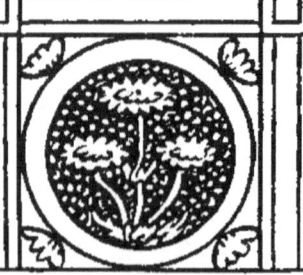

THE SIX SWANS

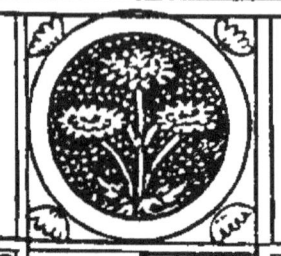

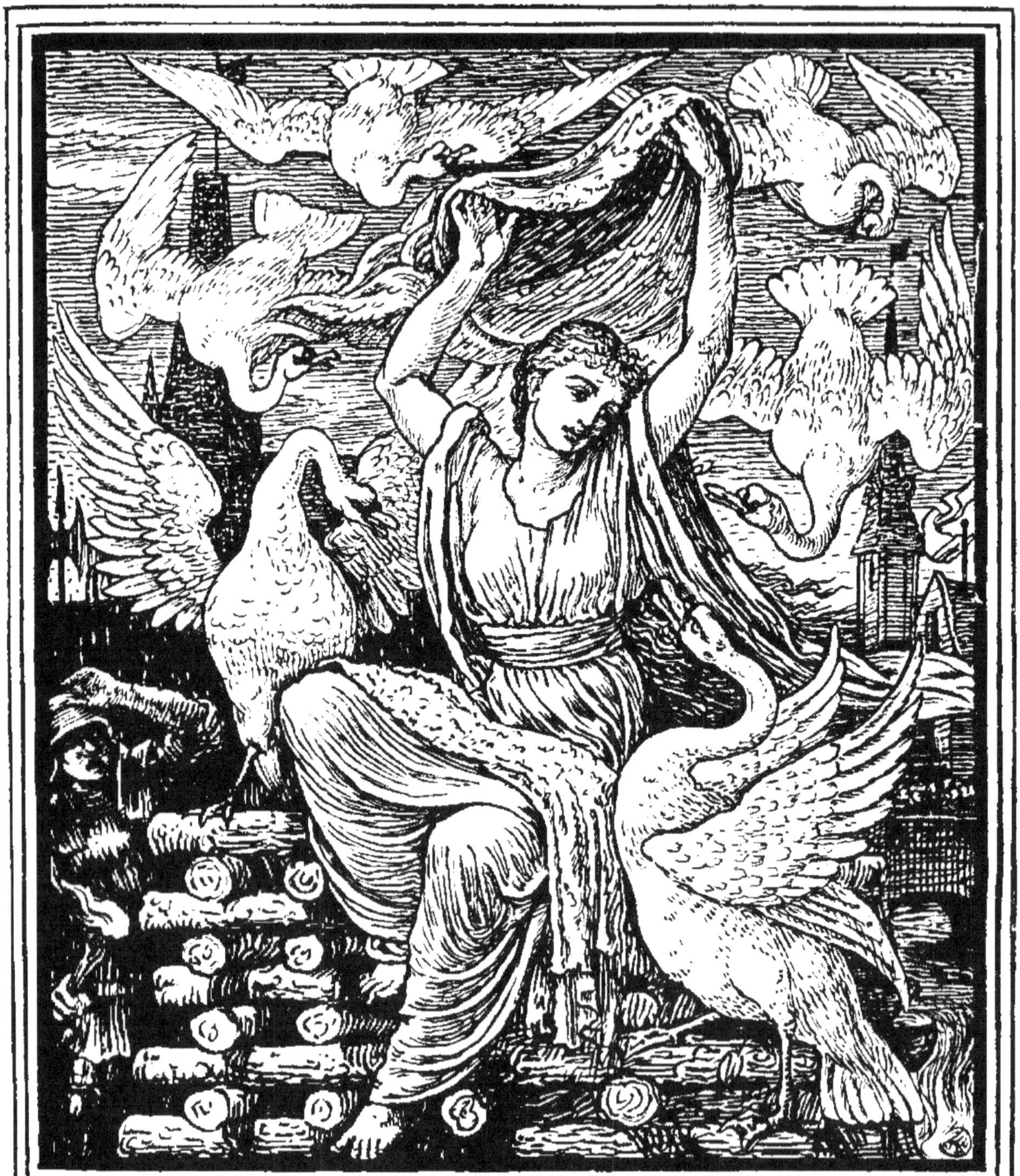

THE SWANS CAME CLOSE UP TO
HER WITH RUSHING WINGS, &
STOOPED ROUND HER, SO THAT
SHE COULD THROW THE SHIRTS
OVER THEM."

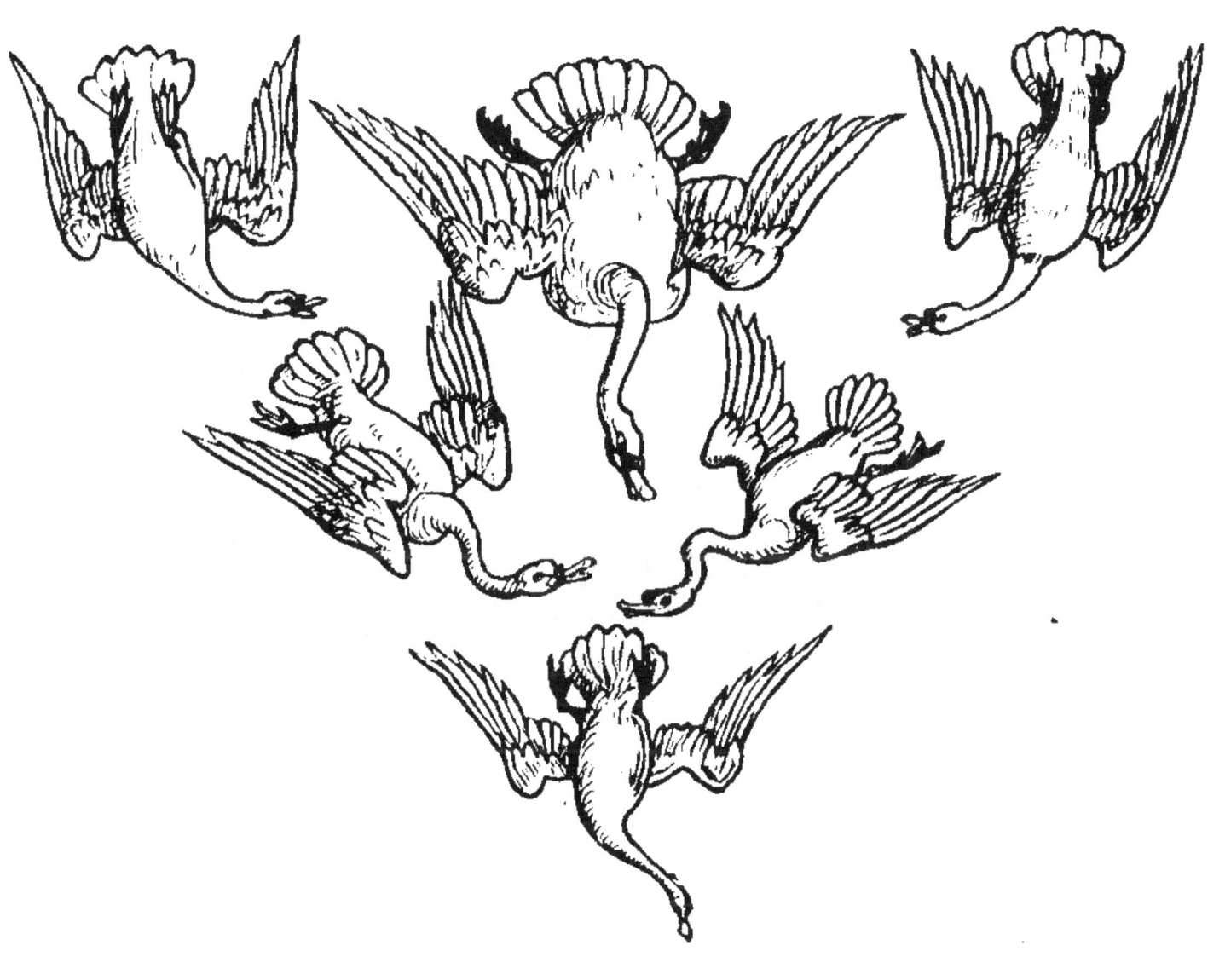

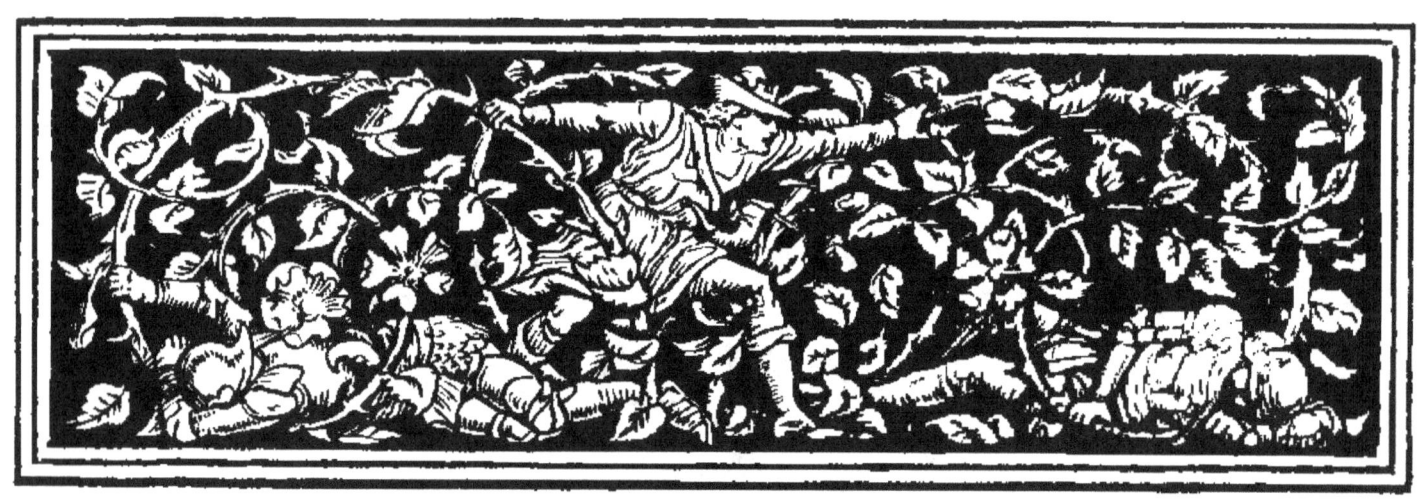

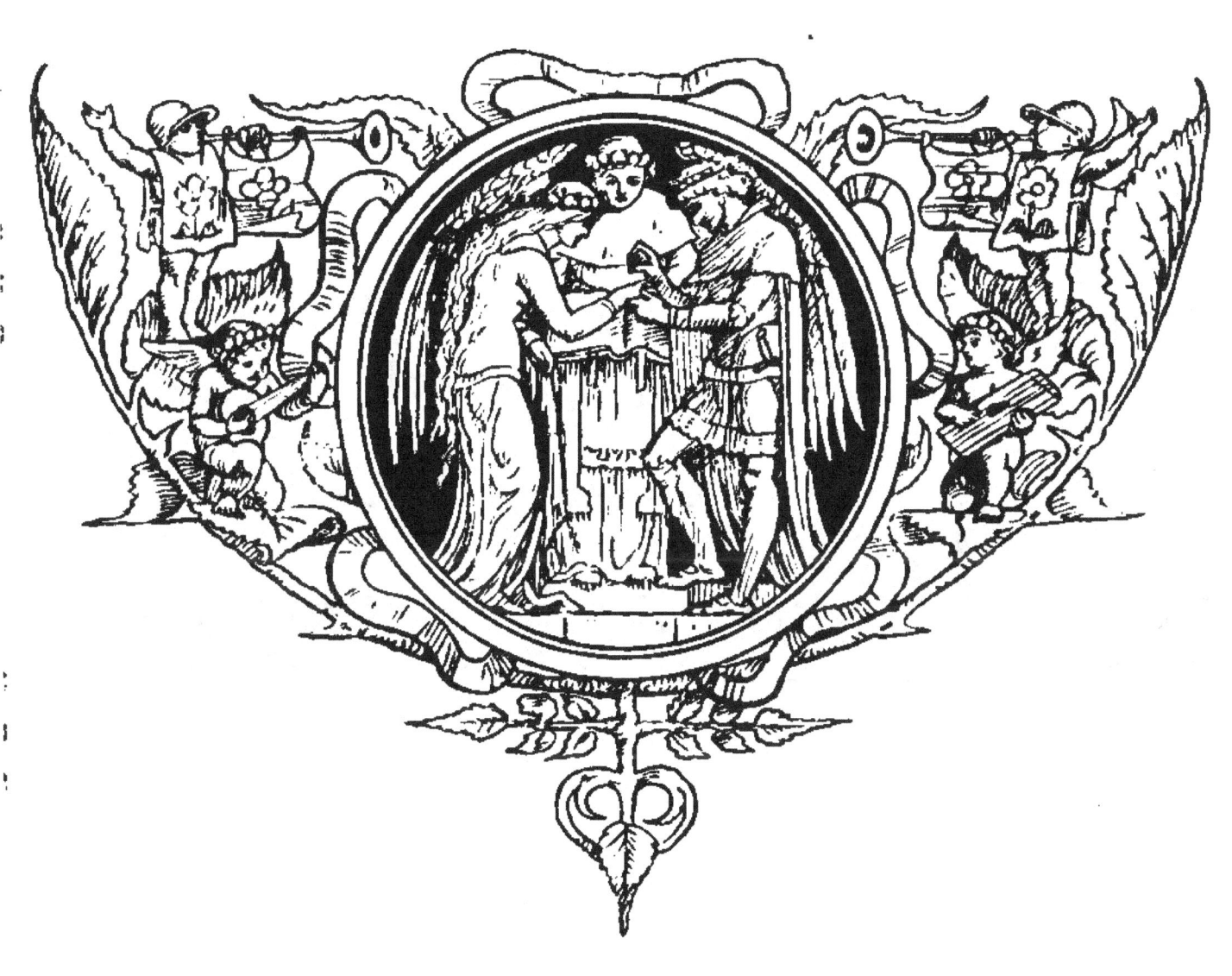

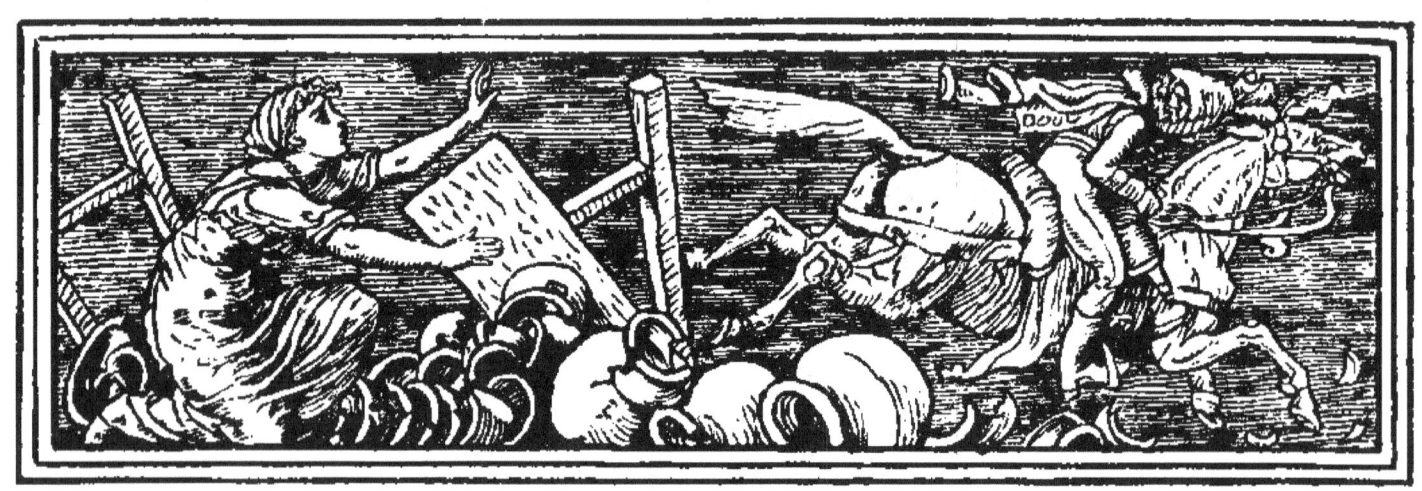